We present to you today the best.

Welcome to the world of air fryer vegetarian cooking! This recipe book has been specially curated for those who are looking for healthy, delicious, and easy-to-prepare vegetarian meals. With the help of an air fryer, you can enjoy your favorite plant-based dishes in a quick, convenient, and healthier way.

Gone are the days of deep-frying or roasting your vegetables to achieve a crispy and golden exterior. The air fryer uses rapid hot air to cook your food, giving it the same crunchy texture without all the added oil and fats. This means you can enjoy your favorite vegetarian dishes without sacrificing taste or sacrificing your health.

In this book, you will find a diverse collection of vegetarian recipes, ranging from appetizers, main dishes, and desserts, all cooked to perfection in an air fryer. Whether you are a seasoned vegetarian or new to plant-based eating, this book has something for everyone. Each recipe includes easy-to-follow instructions, and the end result is always a delicious, healthy, and satisfying meal.

So, get ready to discover the joys of air fryer cooking, and enjoy all your favorite vegetarian dishes in a healthier, tastier, and more convenient way.

Author,

Table of Content

BREAKFAST/ BRUNCH
- *Vegan Casserole* — 3
- *Vegan Bread Roll* — 4
- *Potato Stuff Bread Roll* — 5
- *Breakfast Potatoes* — 6
- *Cauliflower Cakes* — 7
- *Crispy Tofu* — 8
- *Tofu Scramble* — 9
- *Semolina Heart Cutlets* — 10
- *Whole Wheat Toast* — 11
- *Stuffed Cinnamon Toast* — 12
- *Stuffed French Toast* — 13
- *French Toast* — 14
- *Cheese Curds* — 15
- *Basic Bread* — 16
- *Corn Bread* — 17
- *Bread Pudding* — 18
- *Grilled Cheese* — 19
- *Mushroom Cakes* — 20
- *Apple Crisp* — 21

MAIN DISHES
- *Mediterranean Veggies* — 22
- *Roasted Veggies Pasta Salad* — 23
- *Cherry Tomato Salad* — 24
- *Garlic Beans Mix* — 25
- *Green Beans with Shallot* — 26
- *Black Beans & Tomato Chili* — 27
- *Lime Broccoli* — 28
- *Breaded Mushrooms* — 29
- *Zucchini Lasagna Roll-Ups* — 30
- *Sweet Potato Veggie Hash* — 31
- *Crispy Buffalo Cauliflower Bites* — 32
- *Falafel Balls* — 33
- *Stuffed Garlic Mushroom* — 34
- *Sticky Mushroom Rice* — 35
- *Tofu and Cauliflower Rice* — 36
- *Carrot & Potato Mix* — 37
- *Buffalo Tofu* — 38
- *Roasted Carrots* — 39
- *Seaweed Salad with Crispy Tofu* — 40
- *Black Bean- Tomato Soup* — 41
- *Vegan Capprese Sandwiches* — 42
- *Cheesy Vegan Sanwich* — 43
- *Roasted Chickpeas* — 44
- *Simple Vegan Spring Rolls* — 45
- *Cauliflower Rice* — 46
- *Paneer Pizza* — 47
- *Berry Pizza* — 48
- *Pizza Tofu Bites* — 49
- *Thai-Style Veggie Pizza* — 50
- *Mushroom & Pepper Pizza* — 51
- *Potato and Kale Nuggets* — 52
- *Tamarind Glazed Sweet Potatoes* — 53
- *Air Fry Dumplings* — 54
- *Baked Potato With Toppings* — 55

Table of Content

- *Stuffed Eggplant* — 56
- *Garlic-Lemon Tofu* — 57
- *Crispy and Salty Tofu* — 58
- *Panko Tofu* — 59
- *Vegan Sushi Rolls* — 60-61

SIDES, SNACK

- *Crispy Green Tomatoes* — 62
- *Lemon Lentils and Fried Onion* — 63
- *Roasted Kale Chips* — 64
- *Herbed Pita Chips* — 65
- *Lemony Pear Chips* — 66
- *Vegan Popcorn* — 67
- *Crunchy Onion Rings* — 68
- *Simple Potato Chips* — 69
- *Sweet Potato Fries* — 70
- *Crunchy Eggplant Fries* — 71

DESSERTS

- *Chocolate Cake* — 72
- *Coffee Cheesecakes* — 73
- *Lemon Pound Cake* — 74
- *Lime Cheesecake* — 75
- *Sponge Cake* — 76
- *Sweet Potato Cheesecake* — 77
- *Carrot Cake* — 78
- *Cardamom Cakes* — 79
- *Poppyseed Cake* — 80
- *Tangerine Cake* — 81
- *Triple Berry Turnovers* — 82
- *Strawberry Cupcakes* — 83
- *Mini Chocolate Peanut Butter Cupcakes* — 84
- *Maple Cupcakes* — 85
- *Pumpkin Cupcakes* — 86
- *Black Tea Cake* — 87
- *Cranberry Cakes* — 88
- *Chocolate Muffins* — 89
- *Blueberry Muffins* — 90
- *Chocolate Chip Muffins* — 91
- *Oats Muffins* — 92
- *Simple Donuts* — 93
- *Vanilla Mini Donuts* — 94
- *Everything Bagels* — 95
- *Strawberry Donuts* — 96
- *Coconut Donuts* — 97
- *Coffee Donuts* — 98
- *Lemon Poppyseed Donuts* — 99

COOKIES, BREADS, PIES

- *Simple Cookies* — 100
- *Brown Butter Cookies* — 101
- *Potato Chip Cookies* — 102
- *Honey & Oats Cookie* — 103
- *Lentils Cookies* — 104
- *Pumpkin Cookies* — 105
- *Chocolate Chip Cookies* — 106
- *Malted Chocolate Chip Cookie Bars* — 107
- *Lemon Poppy Seed Tea Cookies* — 108

Table of Content

- *Orange Cookies* — 109
- *Trail Mix Cookies* — 110
- *Buttermilk Biscuits* — 111
- *Plum and Currant Tart* — 112
- *Blueberry Tarts* — 113
- *Chocolate Tarts* — 114
- *Strawberry Jam Tarts* — 115
- *Lemon Tart* — 116
- *Fruit Tarts* — 117
- *Banana Bread* — 118
- *Banana Nut Bread* — 119
- *Puff Pastry Cinnamon Swirls* — 120-121
- *Pineapple Squash Bread* — 122
- *Nutella Puff Pastry* — 123
- *Apple Bread* — 124
- *Garlic Bread* — 125
- *Orange Blossoms Bread* — 126-127
- *Strawberry Pie* — 128
- *Pumpkin Pie* — 129
- *Peach Pie* — 130
- *Lentils and Dates Brownies* — 131
- *Vanilla Brownies* — 132

Key Volume Conversions:

1 tablespoon = 3 teaspoons = 15 milliliters
4 tablespoons = 1/4 cup = 60 milliliters
1 ounce = 2 tablespoons = 30 milliliters
1 cup = 8 oz. = 250 milliliters
1 pint = 2 cups = 500 milliliters
1 quart = 4 cups = 950 milliliters
1 quart = 2 pints = 950 milliliters
1 gallon = 4 quarts = 3800 milliliters = 3.8 liters

Dry Ingredient Equivalents:

1 tablespoon = 3 teaspoons = 15 ml
1/8 cup = 2 tablespoons = 30 ml
1/4 cup = 4 tablespoons = 50 ml
1/3 cup = 5-1/3 tablespoons = 75 ml
1/2 cup = 8 tablespoons = 125 ml
2/3 cup = 10-2/3 tablespoons = 150 ml
3/4 cup = 12 tablespoons = 175 ml
1 cup = 16 tablespoons = 250 ml

Wet Ingredient Equivalents:

1 cup = 8 fluid ounces = 1/2 pint
2 cups = 16 fluid ounces = 1 pint
4 cups = 32 fluid ounces = 2 pints
8 cups = 64 fluid = ounces 4 pint

Benefits of Cooking in Air Fryer

- ☑ *Healthier cooking:* Air fryers use hot air to fry food instead of oil, which can result in healthier meals with less fat and calories.

- ☑ *Quick cooking:* Air fryers cook food quickly and evenly, making them a convenient option for busy individuals who want to prepare a meal in a short amount of time.

- ☑ *Energy efficient:* Air fryers use less energy than traditional ovens and stovetops, making them an eco-friendly option for cooking

- ☑ *Versatility:* Air fryers can be used to cook a variety of foods, from crispy french fries and chicken wings to roasted vegetables and baked goods.

- ☑ *Easy to clean:* Most air fryers have non-stick surfaces and are dishwasher safe, making cleanup a breeze.

- ☑ *Reduced kitchen mess:* Because air fryers use hot air instead of oil, they generate less mess and splatter, keeping your kitchen cleaner.

- ☑ *Consistent results:* Air fryers have precise temperature control, ensuring that your food is cooked consistently every time.

Air fryers offer a convenient and healthier way to cook a variety of foods, making them a popular kitchen appliance for those who want to eat well and save time.

Tips for Cooking in Air Fryer

- **_Preheat the air fryer:_** Always preheat the air fryer for a few minutes before cooking to ensure even cooking.

- **_Use nonstick cooking spray:_** To prevent foods from sticking, lightly coat the basket or pan of the air fryer with nonstick cooking spray.

- **_Coat food evenly:_** To ensure even cooking, make sure food is coated evenly. This also helps to achieve crispy results.

- **_Shake and flip food:_** To ensure even cooking, shake the basket occasionally and flip food halfway through the cooking time.

- **_Avoid overcrowding:_** Don't overload the basket of your air fryer, as this can prevent food from cooking evenly.

- **_Use a thermometer:_** To ensure that your baked goods are fully cooked, you should use a thermometer to check the internal temperature of the food.

- **_Use the right cookware:_** Choose cookware that is air fryer-friendly and can withstand high heat, such as heat-resistant silicone or metal.

- **_Experiment with timing:_** Every air fryer is different, so it may take some trial and error to find the perfect cooking time for your specific model.

- **_Keep an eye on food:_** Check food frequently during cooking to prevent it from burning or becoming too crispy.

- **_Use the right temperature:_** Different foods require different temperatures, so be sure to follow the recommended temperature guidelines for your specific recipe.

- **_Keep the basket clean:_** To prevent food from sticking, make sure to clean the basket regularly and avoid using metal utensils that can scratch the non-stick surface.

- The time and temperature may vary slightly depending on the make and model of the air fryer, so you **should consult the manufacturer's instructions and adjust accordingly.**

By following these tips, you will succeed in making delicious meals goods in your air fryer! I wish you success and delicious!

Vegan Casserole

SERVINGS
4

TIME
25 min

DIFFICULTY
Easy

INGREDIENTS

- 2 cups cooked brown rice.
- 2 cups chopped mushrooms.
- 1 large onion, chopped.
- 3 cloves garlic, minced.
- 1 red bell pepper, chopped.
- 1 green bell pepper, chopped.
- 1 can (15 ounces) diced tomatoes.
- 1 can (15 ounces) black beans, rinsed.
- 1 can (15 ounces) corn kernels.
- 2 tablespoons chili powder.
- 1 teaspoon dried oregano.
- Salt and black pepper, to taste.
- 2 cups shredded vegan cheddar cheese.

DIRECTIONS

1. In a pan over medium heat, saute onion, garlic, bell peppers, and mushrooms until the vegetables are tender and the mushrooms have released their liquid, about 8-10 minutes.
2. Stir in the cooked rice, black beans, diced tomatoes, , corn, chili powder, oregano, salt, and pepper.
3. Transfer the mixture to a casserole dish and spread evenly.
4. Sprinkle the shredded vegan cheddar cheese over the top.
5. Preheat the air fryer to 380°F. Bake for 25-30 minutes, or until the cheese is melted and bubbly.
6. Serve hot.

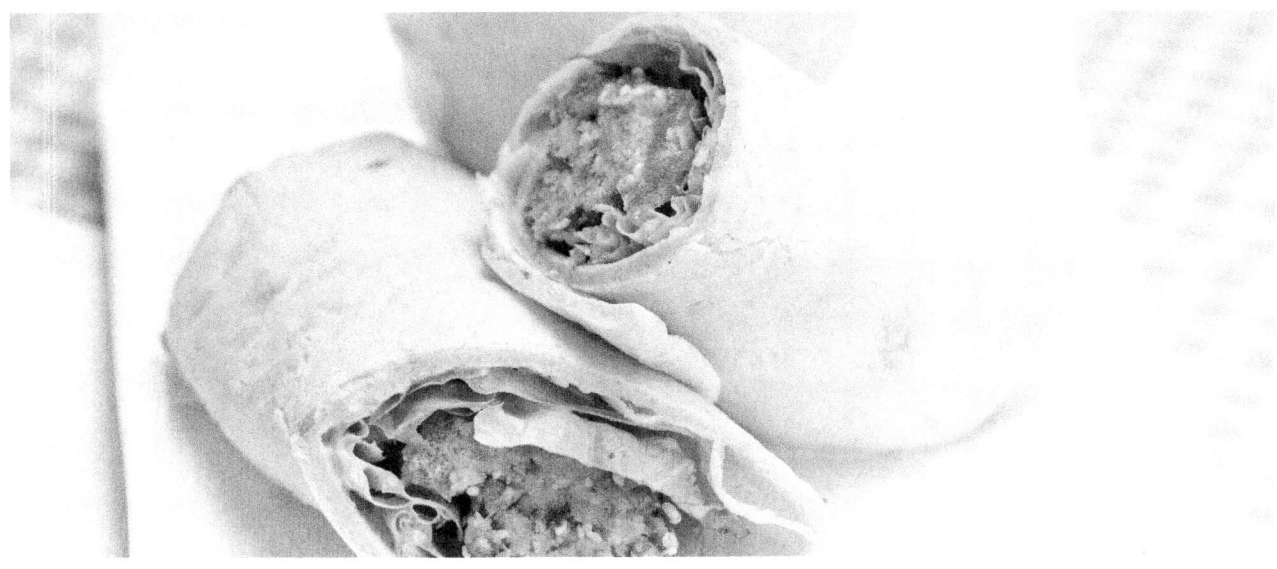

Vegan Bread Roll

SERVINGS	TIME	DIFFICULTY
4	20 min	Easy

INGREDIENTS

- 4 slices of white bread.
- 2 tablespoons finely chopped bell pepper.
- 2 tablespoons vegan butter, softened.
- 2 tablespoons finely chopped onion.
- 1 tablespoon chopped fresh herbs (such as basil or parsley)
- Salt and black pepper, to taste.
- Cooking Spray.

DIRECTIONS

1. Cut the crusts off the bread slices and flatten each slice with a rolling pin. Then spread a thin layer of vegan butter over each slice of bread. Then sprinkle the onion, bell pepper, herbs, salt, and pepper over the butter.
2. Roll up each slice of bread tightly. Brush the rolls lightly with oil.
3. Preheat the air fryer to 380°F. Put the rolls in the air fryer basket, leaving some space between each roll.
4. Air fry to 380°F in 6-8 minutes or until golden brown.
5. Serve warm.

Potato Stuff Bread Roll

SERVINGS
6

TIME
25 min

DIFFICULTY
Easy

INGREDIENTS

- 4 bread slices.
- 2 tablespoons all-purpose flour.
- 2 tablespoons water.
- 2 medium potatoes, boiled and mashed.
- 2 tablespoons finely chopped onion.
- 2 tablespoons chopped cilantro.
- 2 tablespoons finely chopped green chili
- Salt and pepper, to taste.
- Cooking spray.

DIRECTIONS

1. Mix together the mashed potatoes, onion, green chili, cilantro, salt, and pepper in a bowl,
2. Cut the crusts off the bread slices and flatten each slice with a rolling pin. Spoon about 2 tablespoons of the potato mixture onto each bread slice and roll tightly.
3. In another bowl, mix together the flour and water to make a sticky batter. Brush the bread rolls with the batter, making sure to coat all sides evenly.
4. Preheat the air fryer to 400 degrees F for 4 minutes. Then place the rolls in the air fryer basket, leaving some space between each roll. Brush the rolls with a cooking spray.
5. Fry at 400°F for 8-10 minutes or until golden brown. Serve hot.

Breakfast Potatoes

SERVINGS
2

TIME
50 min

DIFFICULTY
Easy

INGREDIENTS

- 1 or 2 large Idaho potatoes
- Aluminum Foil

DIRECTIONS

1. Wash potatoes. Then wrap potatoes in foil.
2. Put potatoes in air fryer basket.
3. Put basket in air fryer and cook at 390° for 50 minutes and serve.

Cauliflower Cakes

SERVINGS
6

TIME
20 min

DIFFICULTY
Easy

INGREDIENTS

- 3.5 cups cauliflower rice.
- 1/4 cup white flour.
- 2 eggs.
- Cooking spray
- 1/2 cup parmesan, grated. Salt and black pepper to the taste.

DIRECTIONS

1. Mix cauliflower rice with salt and pepper in a bowl, stir and squeeze excess water.
2. Transfer cauliflower to other bowl, add eggs, pepper, salt, flour and parmesan, stir really well and shape your cakes.
3. Grease air fryer with cooking spray, heat it up at 400 degrees, add cauliflower cakes and cook them for 10 minutes flipping them halfway.
4. Divide cauliflower cakes on plates and serve.

Crispy Tofu

SERVINGS	TIME	DIFFICULTY
2	15 min	Easy

INGREDIENTS

- 1 block (14-16 ounces) firm tofu, drained.
- 2 tablespoons all-purpose flour.
- 2 tablespoons cornstarch.
- 1 teaspoon smoked paprika.
- 1/2 teaspoon garlic powder.
- Salt and black pepper, to taste.
- Cooking Spray.

DIRECTIONS

1. Cut the tofu into 1-inch cubes.
2. Mix together the cornstarch, flour, paprika, garlic powder, salt, and pepper in a shallow dish. Coat the tofu cubes in the cornstarch mixture, making sure each piece is evenly coated.
3. Place the tofu balls in a single layer in the preheated air fryer basket.
4. Spray the tofu cubes with oil and fry at 400°F for 15-18 minutes, flipping halfway through, or until crispy and golden brown.
5. Serve as desired.

Tofu Scramble

SERVINGS 2

TIME 25 min

DIFFICULTY Easy

INGREDIENTS

- 1 block (14-16 ounces) firm tofu, drained and crumbled.
- 1/2 onion, chopped.
- 1 bell pepper, chopped.
- 2 cloves garlic, minced.
- 2 tablespoons nutritional yeast.
- 1 teaspoon turmeric.
- 2 tablespoons chopped fresh herbs (such as parsley or chives)
- Salt and black pepper, to taste.
- 1 tablespoon oil.

DIRECTIONS

1. Heat the oil in a large pan over medium heat.
2. Add onion, garlic, and bell pepper and saute until tender, about 4 minutes. Add shredded tofu, nutritional yeast, turmeric, salt, and pepper to the pan. Stirred.
3. Pour mixture into baking pan, sprinkle with chopped herbs. Place the baking pan in the preheated air fryer. Fry at 370 degrees F for 5-7 minutes.
4. Serve hot.

Note: You can also add vegetables of your choice, such as mushrooms or spinach, for extra flavor and nutrition.

Semolina Heart Cutlets

SERVINGS 2   **TIME** 25 min   **DIFFICULTY** Easy

INGREDIENTS

- 1 cup semolina.
- 1/2 cup grated carrots.
- 1/2 cup green peas, boiled.
- 2 green chilies, finely chopped.
- 1 inch ginger, grated.
- 2 tablespoons chopped cilantro.
- Salt and black pepper, to taste.
- Cooking Spray.

DIRECTIONS

1. Mix semolina, grated carrot, green beans, green pepper, ginger, cilantro, salt and pepper in a large bowl. Add enough water to the mixture to form a soft dough.
2. Divide the dough into 10-12 equal parts. Shape each portion of the dough into a ball. Flatten it into a round patty.
3. Cut the cake into a heart shape (or not) with a cookie cutter or knife. Repeat with remaining dough.
4. Heat the air fryer to 380 degrees F. Then place the dough pieces in the oiled basket. Fry at 380 degrees F until both sides are golden brown and crispy, about 3-5 minutes per side.
5. Drain on paper towels.
6. Serve hot cutlets with chutney or ketchup of your choice. Enjoy!

Whole Wheat Toast

SERVINGS
6

TIME
15 min

DIFFICULTY
Easy

INGREDIENTS

- 6 slices of whole wheat bread.
- 1.5 tablespoon of vegan butter or margarine, melted.
- Salt and pepper, to taste.
- Cooking Spray.

DIRECTIONS

1. Brush both sides of each slice of bread with melted vegan butter or margarine. Season with salt and pepper to taste.
2. Preheat the air fryer to 400°F then put the slices of bread in a single layer in the air fryer basket.
3. Bake for 4-5 minutes, or until the bread is toasted to your desired level of doneness.
4. Serve hot and enjoy your delicious and healthy vegan toast !

Optional: You can also add toppings like avocado, almond butter, jam, or peanut butter to make your toast more flavorful.

Stuffed Cinnamon Toast

SERVINGS	TIME	DIFFICULTY
4	25 min	Easy

INGREDIENTS

- 2 eggs.
- 1 Slice brioche bread, 2.5 inches thick, preferably stale.
- 4 ounces cream cheese.
- 1 teaspoon cinnamon.
- 2 tablespoons milk.
- 2 tablespoons heavy cream.
- 3 tablespoons sugar.
- 1/2 teaspoon vanilla extract.
- Pistachios, chopped, for topping.
- Maple syrup, for serving.
- Cooking spray.

DIRECTIONS

1. Cut a slit in the middle of the brioche slice, stuff the inside of the slit with cream cheese. Set aside.
2. Whisk together the eggs, milk, heavy cream, sugar, cinnamon, and vanilla extract in a bowl.
3. Soak the stuffed French toast in the egg mixture for 10 seconds on each side. Then Spray each side of the French toast with cooking spray.
4. Place the French toast into the preheated air fryer. Bake in 10 minutes on 350°F.
5. Remove the French toast carefully when done cooking.
6. Top with chopped pistachios and serve with maple syrup.

Stuffed French Toast

SERVINGS	TIME	DIFFICULTY
2	15 min	Easy

INGREDIENTS

- 2 eggs.
- 1 Slice brioche bread, 2.5 inches thick, preferably stale.
- 4 ounces cream cheese.
- 1 teaspoon cinnamon.
- 2 tablespoons milk.
- 2 tablespoons heavy cream.
- 3 tablespoons sugar.
- 1/2 teaspoon vanilla extract.
- Pistachios, chopped, for topping.
- Maple syrup, for serving.
- Cooking spray.

DIRECTIONS

1. Cut a slit in the middle of the brioche slice, stuff the inside of the slit with cream cheese. Set aside.
2. Whisk together the eggs, milk, heavy cream, sugar, cinnamon, and vanilla extract in a bowl.
3. Soak the stuffed French toast in the egg mixture for 10 seconds on each side. Then Spray each side of the French toast with cooking spray.
4. Place the French toast into the preheated air fryer. Bake in 10 minutes on 350°F.
5. Remove the French toast carefully when done cooking.
6. Top with chopped pistachios and serve with maple syrup.

Page 13

French Toast

with Corn Flake Crust, Blueberry Cream Cheese

SERVINGS 4-6   **TIME** 20 min   **DIFFICULTY** Easy

INGREDIENTS

- 2 large eggs, beaten.
- 4 2-inch slices of Challah bread, preferably a few days old.
- 3 teaspoon sugar.
- 1/3 cup whole milk.
- 1/4 teaspoon ground nutmeg.
- 1/4 teaspoon salt.
- 1/4 cup fresh blueberries.
- 4 tablespoons berry-flavored whipped cream cheese.
- 1.5 cups corn flakes, crumbled.

DIRECTIONS

1. In a bowl, mix the egg, milk, sugar, nutmeg and salt.
2. Combine the blueberries and whipped cream cheese in another bowl.
3. Cut a slit into the top crust of each slice of bread. Using a spoon, stuff each piece of bread with 2 tablespoons of berry mixture.
4. Soak each slice of bread in the egg mixture until the entire slice is covered.
5. Place the corn flakes on a plate. Press each slice of bread into the corn flake, evenly coating both sides.
6. Place each slice of bread into the air fryer basket.
7. Set temperature to 400 F degrees and set time for 8 minutes.
8. Serve hot with maple syrup and butter.

Cheese Curds

SERVINGS: 4
TIME: 20 min
DIFFICULTY: Easy

INGREDIENTS

- 1/4 cup flour.
- 1/2 teaspoon salt.
- 8 ounces cheddar cheese curds.
- 1/2 cup panko bread crumbs fine.
- 2 eggs beaten.
- 1/4 teaspoon black pepper.
- 1/2 teaspoon cayenne pepper.

DIRECTIONS

1. Mix the flour, salt, pepper and cayenne pepper in a bowl to combine.
2. Spray the air fryer basket with oil.
3. Dip the cheese curds in flour, then egg, then roll in panko and place in the air fryer basket.
4. Repeat until all cheese curds are coated.
5. Bake at 350° F for 4 to 6 minutes, until golden brown on outside. (Start checking them at 3 minutes to make sure they don't melt).

Basic Bread

SERVINGS
2-4

TIME
50 min

DIFFICULTY
Easy

INGREDIENTS

- 1 cup all-purpose flour.
- 1/2 cup warm water.
- 1/2 teaspoon sugar.
- 1 teaspoon instant yeast.
- 1 tablespoon olive oil.
- 1/2 teaspoon salt.

DIRECTIONS

1. Mix flour, yeast, salt and sugar in a bowl. Gradually add warm water and olive oil to dry ingredients, stirring until a paste forms.
2. Spread the dough out onto a surface and knead for a few minutes until smooth.
3. Place dough in a greased bowl, cover with cling film and let rise in a warm place for 30 minutes.
4. Roll out the dough on a light dough surface 1/2 inch thick, cut the dough and shape to any shape you like.
5. Place the dough in the preheated air fryer basket, placing the breads not too thick. Bake at 380°F for 8-10 minutes or until golden brown.
6. Serve warm.

Corn Bread

SERVINGS
4

TIME
40 min

DIFFICULTY
Medium

INGREDIENTS

- 2 eggs.
- 1/2 cup all-purpose flour.
- 1/2 cup yellow cornmeal.
- 1.5 teaspoons baking powder.
- 2 tablespoons sugar.
- 1/2 cup whole milk.
- 1/2 teaspoon kosher salt.
- 1/4 cup vegetable oil.
- 1/2 cup fresh or frozen corn kernels.
- Cooking spray.

DIRECTIONS

1. Whisk all dry ingredients together in a mixing bowl. Lightly beat wet ingredients together in another bowl, then pour over the dry mix and whisk until smooth.
2. Lightly coat an oven-safe dish with non-stick spray; pour in corn bread mixture. Place the dish into the basket, then put the basket and pan into the air fryer.
3. Set temperature to 350 F degrees and set timer for 25 minutes.
4. When timer goes off, check for doneness with a toothpick. If not done, bake 5 minutes longer.
5. When cooking is complete, invert onto a plate and serve.

Bread Pudding

SERVINGS
4

TIME
25 min

DIFFICULTY
Medium

INGREDIENTS

- 1/2 pound white bread, cubed.
- 3 ounces soft butter.
- 3/4 cup milk.
- 2 teaspoons cornstarch.
- 3/4 cup water.
- 5 tablespoons honey.
- 1/2 cup apple, peeled, cored and roughly chopped.
- 2 teaspoons cinnamon powder.
- 1 teaspoon vanilla extract.
- 0.6 cup brown sugar.
- 1,3 cup flour.

DIRECTIONS

1. Mix bread with apple, milk with water, honey, cinnamon, vanilla and cornstarch and beat well in a bowl.
2. In another bowl, mix flour with sugar and butter and stir until you obtain a crumbled mixture.
3. Preheat the air fryer to 350 degrees F for 3 minutes.
4. Press half of the crumble mix on the bottom of your air fryer, add bread and apple mix, add the rest of the crumble and cook everything at 350 degrees F for 20-22 minutes.
5. Divide bread pudding on plates and serve.

Grilled Cheese

SERVINGS	TIME	DIFFICULTY
2	15 min	Easy

INGREDIENTS

- 4 slices white bread.
- 3 tablespoons butter, melted.
- 1/2 cup sharp cheddar Cheese, shredded, divided

DIRECTIONS

1. Brush butter on each side of the bread slices.
2. Split the cheese evenly between 2 slices of bread and top with remaining bread slices to make 2 sandwiches.
3. Place the sandwiches into the preheated air fryer. Bake at 320°F for 5 minutes.
4. Cut diagonally and serve.

Mushroom Cakes

SERVINGS: 8
TIME: 20 min
DIFFICULTY: Easy

INGREDIENTS

- 4 ounces mushrooms, chopped.
- 14 ounces milk.
- 1 yellow onion, chopped.
- 1 tablespoon butter.
- 1/2 teaspoon nutmeg, ground.
- 1.5 tablespoon flour.
- 2 tablespoons olive oil.
- 1 tablespoon bread crumbs.
- Salt and black pepper to the taste.

DIRECTIONS

1. Heat up a pan with the butter over medium heat, add mushrooms and onion, stir, cook for 3 minutes, add flour, stir well again and take off heat.
2. Add milk slowly to the above mixture, then add salt, pepper and nutmeg, stir and leave aside to cool down completely.
3. Mix oil with bread crumbs and whisk in a bowl.
4. Take spoonfuls of the mushroom filling, add to breadcrumbs mix, coat well, shape patties out of this mix, place them in your air fryer's basket and cook at 380 degrees F for 10 minutes.
5. Take out the cake, wait for it to cool down and enjoy.

Apple Crisp

SERVINGS
2

TIME
15 min

DIFFICULTY
Easy

INGREDIENTS

- 1/4 cup all-purpose flour.
- 4 medium apples, peeled and sliced.
- 1/4 cup granulated sugar.
- 1/4 cup brown sugar.
- 1 teaspoon cinnamon.
- 1/4 teaspoon nutmeg.
- 1/4 cup quick oats.
- 1/4 cup cold butter, cubed.
- 1/2 teaspoon vanilla extract.

DIRECTIONS

1. Mix sliced apples, brown sugar, cinnamon, and nutmeg together in a bowl.
2. In another bowl, mix oats, cold butter, flour, granulated sugar, and vanilla extract until crumbly.
3. Pour the apple mixture into a greased baking tray, then top with the oat mixture.
4. Place the tray in the air fryer basket and cook at 380°F for 15-20 minutes or until the top is golden brown.
5. Serve hot with a scoop of vanilla ice cream or some caramel sauce, if desired. This air fryer deep-fried apple is a sweet and satisfying dessert that's perfect for any occasion. Enjoy!

Mediterranean Veggies

SERVINGS	TIME	DIFFICULTY
2	15 min	Easy

INGREDIENTS

- 1 red onion, sliced.
- 1 yellow bell pepper, sliced.
- 1 red bell pepper, sliced.
- 1 zucchini, sliced.
- 1 eggplant, sliced.
- 2 tbsp olive oil.
- 1 tsp dried oregano.
- 1 tsp dried basil.
- Salt and pepper to taste.

DIRECTIONS

1. Mix together the sliced zucchini, eggplant, bell peppers, and onion in a large bowl. Add the olive oil, oregano, basil, salt, and pepper to the bowl and mix to combine.
2. Preheat air fryer to 400°F. Place the vegetables in a single layer in the air fryer basket, making sure they are not crowded. Fry for 10-15 minutes, flipping the vegetables halfway through, until they are tender and golden.
3. Serve as a side dish or over rice or quinoa.

Roasted Veggies Pasta Salad

SERVINGS	TIME	DIFFICULTY
2	20 min	Easy

INGREDIENTS

- 200g pasta.
- 1 red bell pepper, sliced.
- 1 yellow bell pepper, sliced.
- 1 red onion, sliced.
- 1 cup cherry tomatoes, halved.
- 1 garlic, minced.
- 1 tsp dried basil.
- 1/4 cup freshly grated parmesan cheese.
- 2 tbsp freshly squeezed lemon juice.
- 2 tbsp balsamic vinegar.
- 2 tbsp olive oil.
- Salt and pepper to taste.

DIRECTIONS

1. Cook the pasta according to package instructions. Drain and rinse with cold water.
2. Mix together the sliced bell peppers, onion, garlic, cherry tomatoes, olive oil, basil, salt, and pepper in a large bowl,
3. Preheat air fryer to 400°F. Place the vegetables in a single layer in the air fryer basket, making sure they are not crowded. Fry for 10-15 minutes, flipping the vegetables halfway through, until they are tender and golden.
4. In a serving bowl, combine the cooked pasta with the roasted vegetables. Add the parmesan cheese, lemon juice, and balsamic vinegar to the pasta and vegetables and mix to combine.
5. Serve the pasta salad warm or chilled.

Cherry Tomato Salad

SERVINGS
2

TIME
20 min

DIFFICULTY
Easy

INGREDIENTS

- 1 pint cherry tomatoes, cut halved.
- 1 tbsp olive oil.
- 1 tbsp balsamic vinegar.
- 1 tbsp chopped fresh basil.
- Salt and pepper to taste.

DIRECTIONS

1. Mix together the cherry tomatoes, olive oil, salt, and pepper in a large bowl.
2. Preheat the air fryer to 400°F. Place the cherry tomato mixture in the air fryer basket in a single layer. Cook for 8-10 minutes, or until the tomatoes are slightly softened and charred.
3. Remove the tomatoes from the air fryer and transfer to a serving dish. Drizzle with balsamic vinegar and sprinkle with chopped basil.
4. Serve the cherry tomato salad warm or at room temperature.

Garlic Beans Mix

SERVINGS
2

TIME
20 min

DIFFICULTY
Easy

INGREDIENTS

- 1 lb green beans, trimmed.
- 1 lb baby carrots.
- 4 cloves garlic, minced.
- 2 tbsp olive oil.
- Salt and pepper to taste.

DIRECTIONS

1. Mix together the green beans, baby carrots, olive oil, garlic, salt, and pepper in a large bowl.
2. Preheat the air fryer to 400°F. Place the green bean and carrot mixture in the air fryer basket in a single layer. Cook for 12-15 minutes, or until the vegetables are tender and slightly charred.
3. Remove the vegetables from the air fryer and transfer to a serving dish.
4. Serve the garlic bean mix warm.

Green Beans with Shallot

 SERVINGS
2

 TIME
20 min

DIFFICULTY
Easy

INGREDIENTS

- 1 lb fresh green beans, trimmed.
- 1 tbsp olive oil.
- 1 large shallot, thinly sliced.
- Salt and pepper to taste.

DIRECTIONS

1. Combine the green beans, shallot, olive oil, salt, and pepper in a bowl.
2. Preheat the air fryer to 400°F. Place the mixture in the air fryer basket in a single layer.
3. Cook for 12-15 minutes, tossing occasionally, until the green beans are tender and slightly charred.
4. Remove the green beans from the air fryer and serve hot.

Black Beans & Tomato Chili

SERVINGS 2 | **TIME** 20 min | **DIFFICULTY** Easy

INGREDIENTS

- 2 cups canned black beans, drained and rinsed.
- 1 tbsp olive oil.
- 3 cloves garlic, minced.
- 1 large onion, chopped.
- 1 tsp chili powder.
- 1 large tomato, chopped.
- 1 tsp cumin.
- Salt and pepper to taste.

DIRECTIONS

1. Mix together the olive oil, onion, garlic, black beans, tomato, chili powder, cumin, salt, and pepper in a large bowl.
2. Preheat the air fryer to 400°F. Pour the mixture into the air fryer basket. Cook for 15-20 minutes, stirring occasionally, until the vegetables are tender and the mixture is heated through.
3. Serve hot, topped with shredded cheese, sour cream, or any other desired toppings.

Lime Broccoli

SERVINGS
2

TIME
20 min

DIFFICULTY
Easy

INGREDIENTS

- 1 lb broccoli florets.
- 1 lime, juiced.
- Salt and pepper to taste.
- 1 tsp chili powder.
- 2 tbsp olive oil.
- 1 tsp cumin.

DIRECTIONS

1. Mix together the broccoli florets, olive oil, lime juice, salt, pepper, chili powder, and cumin in a large bowl.
2. Preheat the air fryer to 380°F. Place the broccoli mixture in the air fryer basket in a single layer. Fry for 14-16 minutes, or until the broccoli is tender and slightly charred.
3. Remove the broccoli from the air fryer and transfer to a serving dish.
4. Serve the lime broccoli warm

Breaded Mushrooms

SERVINGS
2

TIME
20 min

DIFFICULTY
Easy

INGREDIENTS

- 1 head of cauliflower.
- 1 tablespoon olive oil.
- Salt and pepper to taste.
- Seasonings: garlic powder, onion powder, paprika...

DIRECTIONS

1. In a first shallow dish, mix together the flour, salt, pepper, and any optional seasonings.
2. In a second shallow dish, beat the eggs. In a third shallow dish, mix together the breadcrumbs.
3. Dredge each mushroom in the flour mixture, then dip it into the beaten eggs, and finally coat it in the breadcrumbs.
4. Preheat your air fryer to 400°F. Lightly spray the air fryer basket with cooking spray.
5. Place the coated mushrooms in a single layer in the air fryer basket, making sure they are not crowded. Fry for 10-12 minutes, flipping the mushrooms halfway through, until they are golden and crispy on the outside. Serve and Enjoy!

Zucchini Lasagna Roll-Ups

SERVINGS
2

TIME
20 min

DIFFICULTY
Medium

INGREDIENTS

- 1 egg.
- 4 large zucchini. Cut off the ends, slice them lengthwise into 0.25-inch slices.
- 1 cup marinara sauce.
- 1 tsp dried basil.
- 1 tsp dried oregano.
- 1 cup ricotta cheese.
- 1/4 cup grated Parmesan cheese.
- 1 cup shredded mozzarella cheese.
- Salt and pepper, to taste.
- Cooking spray.

DIRECTIONS

1. In a mixing bowl, mix together the mozzarella cheese, ricotta cheese, Parmesan cheese, egg, basil, oregano, salt, and pepper.
2. Preheat your air fryer to 400°F. Spread a thin layer of marinara sauce on the bottom of the air fryer basket.
3. Spoon a small amount of the cheese mixture onto each zucchini slice, spreading it evenly. Roll up the zucchini slices, starting from one end and rolling to the other.
4. Place the zucchini roll-ups seam-side down in the air fryer basket, making sure they are not touching.
5. Lightly spray the tops of the roll-ups with non-stick cooking spray. Cook in the preheated air fryer for 12-15 minutes, or until the cheese is melted and the zucchini is tender.
6. Serve the zucchini lasagna roll-ups hot with additional marinara sauce and grated Parmesan cheese, if like.

Sweet Potato Veggie Hash

SERVINGS
2

TIME
20 min

DIFFICULTY
Easy

INGREDIENTS

- 1 large sweet potato, peeled and diced.
- 1 cup cherry tomatoes, halved.
- 1 red bell pepper, diced.
- 1 yellow onion, diced.
- 1 tablespoon olive oil.
- 1 tsp paprika.
- 1 tsp garlic powder.
- Salt and pepper, to taste.

DIRECTIONS

1. In a large bowl, toss the sweet potato, bell pepper, onion, cherry tomatoes, olive oil, salt, pepper, paprika, and garlic powder together until everything is evenly coated.
2. Preheat the air fryer to 400°F. Place the vegetable mixture in the air fryer basket in an even layer. Cook for 15-18 minutes, or until the vegetables are tender and slightly charred, flipping once halfway through.
3. Serve the veggie hash hot, topped with your favorite seasonings and/or toppings.

Crispy Buffalo Cauliflower Bites

SERVINGS
2

TIME
20 min

DIFFICULTY
Easy

INGREDIENTS

- 1 cup all-purpose flour.
- 1 head of cauliflower, cut into florets.
- 1 cup water.
- 1 tsp garlic powder.
- 1 tsp paprika.
- 1 tsp dried oregano.
- 1/2 cup hot sauce.
- 1 tbsp unsalted butter, melted.
- Salt and pepper, to taste.
- Cooking spray.

DIRECTIONS

1. Whisk together the flour, garlic powder, paprika, oregano, salt, and pepper in a large mixing bowl.
2. In another bowl, whisk together the water, hot sauce, and melted butter.
3. Dip each cauliflower floret into the flour mixture, then into the hot sauce mixture, then back into the flour mixture.
4. Preheat the air fryer to 400°F. Lightly spray the air fryer basket with non-stick cooking spray. Place the coated cauliflower florets in the air fryer basket in a single layer. Fry for 15-18 minutes, or until the cauliflower is crispy and golden brown, flipping once halfway through.
5. Serve with your favorite dipping sauce.

Falafel Balls

SERVINGS	TIME	DIFFICULTY
2	25 min	Medium

INGREDIENTS

- 2 tbsp flour.
- 2 tbsp olive oil.
- 1 can of chickpeas, drained and rinsed.
- 1 tsp ground cumin.
- 1 tsp ground coriander.
- 1/2 cup parsley leaves.
- 1/2 cup cilantro leaves.
- 1 small onion, chopped.
- 3 cloves of garlic, minced.
- 1/2 tsp baking powder.
- Salt and pepper to taste.

DIRECTIONS

1. In a food processor, combine the chickpeas, parsley, cilantro, onion, garlic, cumin, coriander, baking powder, salt, pepper, flour, and olive oil. Pulse until a smooth dough forms.
2. Scoop the dough into tablespoon-sized balls and flatten them slightly into patties.
3. Preheat the air fryer to 380°F. Then place the falafel balls in the air fryer basket in a single layer. Fry for 12-15 minutes or until the falafel balls are crispy and golden brown.
4. Remove the falafel balls from the air fryer and transfer to a serving dish.
5. Serve the falafel balls warm with your favorite dipping sauce.

Stuffed Garlic Mushroom

SERVINGS	TIME	DIFFICULTY
8	20 min	Easy

INGREDIENTS

- 8-10 large mushrooms, clean and remove the stems.
- 1/4 cup breadcrumbs.
- 1/4 cup grated Parmesan cheese.
- 1 tbsp butter, melted.
- 1 tbsp olive oil.
- 2 cloves of garlic, minced.
- 1/4 cup chopped fresh parsley.
- Salt and pepper to taste.

DIRECTIONS

1. Mix together the olive oil, garlic, breadcrumbs, Parmesan cheese, parsley, salt, pepper, and melted butter in a small bowl. Fill each mushroom cap with the breadcrumb mixture.
2. Preheat the air fryer to 400°F. Then place the stuffed mushroom caps in the air fryer basket in a single layer. Cook for 12-15 minutes, or until the mushrooms are tender and the filling is golden brown.
3. Remove the mushrooms from the air fryer and serve hot. Enjoy!

Sticky Mushroom Rice

SERVINGS 2 | **TIME** 25 min | **DIFFICULTY** Easy

INGREDIENTS

- 1.5 cups rice.
- 2 cups water.
- 1 tbsp vegetable oil.
- 1 tbsp rice vinegar.
- 2 cloves of garlic, minced.
- 3 tbsp soy sauce.
- 1 cup sliced mushrooms.
- 2 tbsp brown sugar.
- 1 tsp cornstarch.
- 2 tbsp water.
- Salt and pepper to taste.

DIRECTIONS

1. Rinse the rice and add it to the air fryer basket with the 2 cups of water. Cook the rice for 15-18 minutes or until tender.
2. In a large pan, heat the oil over medium heat. Add the garlic and mushrooms and cook for 3-4 minutes, or until the mushrooms are tender.
3. In a bowl, whisk together the soy sauce, brown sugar, rice vinegar, cornstarch, and 2 tbsp of water. Pour the mixture over the mushrooms and stir to combine.
4. Cook for 2-3 minutes, or until the sauce has thickened.
5. Serve the sticky mushroom mixture over the cooked rice. Enjoy!

Tofu and Cauliflower Rice

SERVINGS: 2
TIME: 20 min
DIFFICULTY: Easy

INGREDIENTS

- 1 block of firm tofu, drained and pressed.
- 1 head of cauliflower, grated.
- 1 tbsp olive oil.
- 1 tsp garlic powder.
- 1 tsp onion powder.
- 1 tsp chili powder.
- 1 tsp paprika.
- Salt and pepper to taste.

DIRECTIONS

1. Mix together the grated cauliflower, olive oil, garlic powder, onion powder, chili powder, paprika, salt, and pepper in a large bowl.
2. Preheat the air fryer to 400°F then place the mixture in the air fryer basket in a single layer. Cook for 12-15 minutes, or until the cauliflower is tender and lightly browned.
3. Cut the tofu into 1-inch cubes.
4. Place the tofu in the air fryer basket in a single layer. Fry for 10-12 minutes, or until the tofu is crispy and golden brown.
5. Serve the tofu over the cauliflower rice.

Carrot & Potato Mix

SERVINGS
6

TIME
20 min

DIFFICULTY
Easy

INGREDIENTS

- 2 medium carrots, sliced.
- 2 medium potatoes, sliced.
- 1 tsp dried thyme.
- 1 tbsp olive oil.
- Salt and pepper to taste.

DIRECTIONS

1. Mix together the carrots, potatoes, olive oil, thyme, salt, and pepper in a large bowl.
2. Preheat the air fryer to 400°F. Place the mixture in the air fryer basket in a single layer.
3. Cook for 20-25 minutes, or until the vegetables are tender and lightly browned.
4. Serve the roasted carrot and potato mix immediately. Enjoy!

Buffalo Tofu

SERVINGS | TIME | DIFFICULTY
6 | 20 min | Easy

INGREDIENTS

- 1/2 cup flour.
- 1 block of firm tofu, drained and pressed.
- 1 tsp garlic powder.
- 1 tsp onion powder.
- 1/2 cup water.
- 1/2 cup hot sauce (such as Frank's RedHot)
- 2 tbsp unsalted butter (or vegan butter)
- Salt and pepper to taste.

DIRECTIONS

1. Cut the tofu into 1-inch cubes.
2. Mix together the flour, garlic powder, onion powder, salt, and pepper in a large bowl. Dip each tofu cube in the flour mixture to coat.
3. Preheat the air fryer to 400°F. Place the coated tofu cubes in the air fryer basket in a single layer.
4. Fry for 10-12 minutes, or until the tofu is crispy and golden brown. (Flip them in half the time)
5. In a separate bowl, whisk together the water, hot sauce, and butter.
6. Toss the cooked tofu cubes in the hot sauce mixture to coat. Serve hot.

Roasted Carrots

SERVINGS
6

TIME
20 min

DIFFICULTY
Easy

INGREDIENTS

- 1 lb baby carrots.
- 1 tbsp olive oil.
- 1 tsp dried thyme.
- Salt and pepper to taste.

DIRECTIONS

1. Mix together the carrots, olive oil, thyme, salt, and pepper in a large bowl.
2. Preheat the air fryer to 400°F. Place the mixture in the air fryer basket in a single layer. Bake for 12-15 minutes, or until the carrots are tender and lightly browned.
3. Serve the roasted carrots immediately. Enjoy!

Seaweed Salad with Crispy Tofu

SERVINGS
2

TIME
20 min

DIFFICULTY
Easy

INGREDIENTS

For the Seaweed Salad:
- 2 cups seaweed, rinsed and drained.
- 1 tsp sugar.
- 1 tsp sesame seeds.
- 1 tbsp rice vinegar.
- 1 tbsp soy sauce.
- 1 tsp sesame oil.
- Salt and pepper to taste.

For the Crispy Tofu:
- 1 block of firm tofu, drained and pressed.
- 1 tbsp olive oil.
- 1 tbsp cornstarch.
- Salt and pepper to taste.

DIRECTIONS

For the Seaweed Salad:
1. Mix together the seaweed, rice vinegar, sesame oil, soy sauce, sugar, sesame seeds, salt, and pepper in a large bowl.
2. Set aside the seaweed salad while you prepare the crispy tofu.

For the Crispy Tofu:
1. Cut the tofu into 0.5-inch cubes.
2. In a large dish, toss the tofu with the cornstarch, olive oil, salt, and pepper until evenly coated.
3. Preheat the air fryer to 380°F. Place the tofu in the air fryer basket in a single layer. Fry for 12-15 minutes, or until the tofu is crispy and golden brown.
4. Serve the seaweed salad with the crispy tofu on top. Enjoy!

Black Bean- Tomato Soup
(With Pobland Chili Rings)

SERVINGS	TIME	DIFFICULTY
2	25 min	Medium

INGREDIENTS

- 1 can of black beans, drained and rinsed.
- 1 small onion, chopped.
- 2 medium tomatoes, chopped.
- 2 cloves of garlic, minced.
- 1 tsp chili powder.
- 1 tsp cumin.
- 2 cups vegetable broth.
- Salt and pepper to taste.

The Poblano Chili Rings:
- 2 large poblano chili. peppers, sliced into rings.
- 2 tbsp olive oil.
- Salt to taste.

DIRECTIONS

For the Soup:
1. In a blender, puree the black beans, tomatoes, onion, garlic, vegetable broth, salt, pepper, chili powder, and cumin until smooth.
2. Pour the pureed soup into a large saucepan and cook over medium heat for 5 minutes, or until heated through.

For the Poblano Chili Rings:
1. Toss the poblano chili pepper rings with the olive oil and salt in a large bowl.
2. Preheat the air fryer to 400°F. Place the chili pepper rings in the air fryer basket in a single layer. Fry for 8-10 minutes or until the chili rings are slightly charred and tender.
3. Serve the black bean-tomato soup with the poblano chili rings on top.

Vegan Capprese Sandwiches

SERVINGS	TIME	DIFFICULTY
4	20 min	Medium

INGREDIENTS

- 4 vegan focaccia buns.
- 1/2 cup vegan mozzarella cheese, shredded.
- 1/2 cup basil leaves.
- 1 large tomato, sliced.
- 1/4 cup balsamic glaze.
- 2 tbsp olive oil.
- Salt and pepper to taste.

DIRECTIONS

1. Preheat the air fryer to 380°F.
2. Cut each focaccia bun in half horizontally and place one half, cut side up, in the air fryer basket.
3. Spoon some of the vegan mozzarella cheese onto the bottom half of each focaccia bun. Top each bun with tomato slices and basil leaves. Season with salt and pepper to taste.
4. Put the other half of the focaccia bun on top and brush with olive oil.
5. Bake for 4-6 minutes or until the cheese is melted.
6. Remove the capprese sandwiches from the air fryer and drizzle with balsamic glaze.
7. Serve warm.

Cheesy Vegan Sanwich

SERVINGS
4

TIME
20 min

DIFFICULTY
Medium

INGREDIENTS

- 2 slices of vegan bread.
- 2 tbsp butter.
- 2 tbsp cream cheese.
- 2 tbsp shredded cheese.
- 4 slices of avocado.
- Salt and pepper to taste.

DIRECTIONS

1. Spread the vegan cream cheese on one slice of the vegan bread. Sprinkle the vegan shredded cheese on top of the cream cheese. Layer the avocado slices on top of the cheese. Season with salt and pepper to taste.
2. Put the other slice of vegan bread on top of the avocado to make a sandwich. Spread the butter on the outside of the sandwich.
3. Preheat the air fryer to 400°F. Place the sandwich in the air fryer basket.
4. Cook for 3-5 minutes or until the cheese is melted and the bread is toasted.
5. Remove and serve hot.

Roasted Chickpeas

SERVINGS
2

TIME
20 min

DIFFICULTY
Medium

INGREDIENTS

- 2 cans of chickpeas, drained and rinsed.
- 1 tsp chili powder.
- 2 tbsp olive oil.
- 1 tsp cumin.
- Salt and pepper to taste.

DIRECTIONS

1. Mix together the chickpeas, olive oil, salt, pepper, chili powder, and cumin In a large bowl.
2. Preheat the air fryer to 400°F. Then place the chickpeas in the air fryer basket in a single layer.
3. Cook for 12-15 minutes, or until the chickpeas are crispy and slightly charred.
4. Remove the chickpeas from the air fryer and transfer to a serving dish.
5. Serve the roasted chickpeas warm.

Simple Vegan Spring Rolls

SERVINGS
2

TIME
20 min

DIFFICULTY
Medium

INGREDIENTS

- 8 spring roll wrappers.
- 1 cup chopped mushrooms.
- 2 cups shredded carrots.
- 1 cup chopped cabbage.
- 2 cloves garlic, minced.
- 1/2 cup chopped scallions.
- Salt and pepper to taste.
- Oil for brushing.

DIRECTIONS

1. Mix together the carrots, cabbage, mushrooms, scallions, garlic, salt, and pepper in a large bowl.
2. Place about 2 tablespoons of the mixture onto each spring roll wrapper. Roll up the wrapper tightly, sealing the edges.
3. Preheat the air fryer to 400°F. Brush the spring rolls with a little oil. Place the spring rolls in the air fryer basket in a single layer. Fry for 10-12 minutes, or until the spring rolls are golden and crispy.
4. Serve the spring rolls with your favorite dipping sauce.

Cauliflower Rice

SERVINGS
2

TIME
20 min

DIFFICULTY
Easy

INGREDIENTS

- 1 head of cauliflower.
- 1 tablespoon olive oil.
- Salt and pepper to taste.
- Seasonings: garlic powder, onion powder, paprika...

DIRECTIONS

1. Cut the cauliflower into florets and place them in a food processor. Pulse until the cauliflower is broken down into rice-sized pieces.
2. Mix together the cauliflower rice, olive oil, salt, pepper, and any optional seasonings in a bowl,
3. Preheat your air fryer to 400°F. Place the mixture in a single layer in the air fryer basket, making sure it is not crowded.
4. Fry for 10-12 minutes, stirring halfway through, until the cauliflower is tender and lightly browned.
5. Serve the cauliflower rice as a side dish or as a base for a stir-fry.

Paneer Pizza

SERVINGS 4 | **TIME** 20 min | **DIFFICULTY** Medium

INGREDIENTS

- 1 pre-made pizza crust.
- 1/2 cup pizza sauce.
- 1/2 cup sliced onions.
- 1/2 cup sliced bell peppers.
- 1/2 cup sliced mushrooms.
- 1 cup shredded mozzarella cheese.
- 1 cup crumbled paneer cheese.
- Salt and pepper to taste.

DIRECTIONS

1. Place the pizza crust on a piece of parchment paper. Spread the pizza sauce evenly over the crust, leaving a 1/2-inch border around the edges. Sprinkle the mozzarella cheese over the sauce.
2. Add the paneer cheese, onions, bell peppers, and mushrooms on top of the cheese. Sprinkle salt and pepper over the toppings.
3. Preheat your air fryer to 400°F. Place the parchment paper with the pizza in the air fryer basket, bake for 8-10 minutes, or until the crust is golden and the cheese is melted.
4. Remove the pizza from the air fryer and let it cool for a few minutes before slicing and serving.

Berry Pizza

SERVINGS
1

TIME
25 min

DIFFICULTY
Easy

INGREDIENTS

- 1 ready-made pizza crust.
- 2 tablespoons of butter.
- 2 tablespoons of granulated sugar.
- 1/4 cup of cream cheese, softened.
- 2 tablespoons of honey.
- 1 teaspoon of vanilla extract.
- 1/2 cup of mixed berries (such as blueberries, raspberries, and blackberries)
- 1 tablespoon of cornstarch.
- 1 tablespoon of lemon juice.
- Powdered sugar, for dusting.

DIRECTIONS

1. Heat the air fryer to 400°F (200°C).
2. Place the pizza base in the air fryer basket and cook for 5 minutes.
3. In a small bowl, whisk together cream cheese, honey, and vanilla extract. Then spread the cream cheese mixture evenly over the cooked pizza crust.
4. In another small bowl, whisk together the berries, sugar, cornstarch, and lemon juice.
5. Spoon the berry mixture over the cream cheese mixture.
6. Dot the berry mixture with small pieces of butter.
7. Bake the berry pizza in the air fryer for an additional 10-12 minutes or until the crust is golden brown.
8. Remove from the air fryer and let cool for a few minutes. Sprinkle with powdered sugar and serve.

Pizza Tofu Bites

SERVINGS
6

TIME
15 min

DIFFICULTY
Easy

INGREDIENTS

- 1 block of firm tofu, drained and cut into bite-sized cubes.
- 1 teaspoon of dried oregano.
- 1 teaspoon of dried basil.
- 1/2 cup of tomato sauce.
- 1/2 cup of shredded mozzarella cheese.
- 1/4 cup of grated parmesan cheese.
- 1/2 teaspoon of garlic powder.
- Salt and pepper, to taste.
- 1 tablespoon of olive oil.

DIRECTIONS

1. Mix together the tofu cubes, tomato sauce, mozzarella cheese, parmesan cheese, oregano, basil, garlic powder, salt, pepper, and olive oil in a large bowl.
2. Preheat the air fryer to 390°F. Put the tofu mixture into the air fryer basket in a single layer.
3. Cook for 10-12 minutes, flipping the tofu bites once during cooking, until they are crispy and golden brown.
4. Serve hot, with additional tomato sauce and grated cheese on top, if desired. Enjoy!

Thai-Style Veggie Pizza

SERVINGS
4

TIME
20 min

DIFFICULTY
Medium

INGREDIENTS

- 1 store-bought pizza crust.
- 1 cup sliced mushrooms.
- 1 cup shredded mozzarella cheese.
- 1 red bell pepper, sliced.
- 1/2 cup peanut sauce.
- 1/2 cup sliced red onion.
- 1/2 cup diced pineapple.
- 1/2 cup shredded carrots.
- 1/2 cup chopped cilantro.

DIRECTIONS

1. Place the pizza crust on a lightly floured surface and spread the peanut sauce evenly over the crust, leaving a 1/2-inch border around the edges.
2. Layer the bell pepper, mushrooms, pineapple, carrots, red onion, and cilantro over the peanut sauce. Sprinkle the mozzarella cheese over the toppings.
3. Preheat the air fryer to 400°F. Place the pizza in the air fryer basket and cook for 8-10 minutes, or until the crust is crispy and the cheese is melted.
4. Serve the pizza hot, garnished with additional cilantro and a sprinkle of red pepper flakes, if desired.

Mushroom & Pepper Pizza

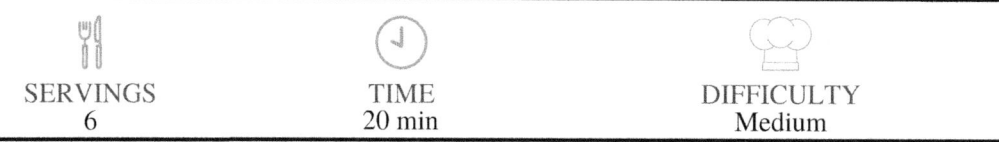

SERVINGS	TIME	DIFFICULTY
6	20 min	Medium

INGREDIENTS

- 1 pre-made pizza crust.
- 1 cup sliced mushrooms.
- 1 red bell pepper, sliced.
- 1 tsp dried oregano.
- 1 cup shredded mozzarella cheese.
- 2 tbsp tomato sauce.
- Salt and pepper to taste.

DIRECTIONS

1. Place the pizza crust in the air fryer basket. Spread the tomato sauce evenly over the crust. Sprinkle the sliced mushrooms and red bell pepper over the sauce. Then sprinkle the shredded mozzarella cheese over the toppings. Sprinkle dried oregano, salt and pepper over the cheese.
2. Preheat the air fryer to 400°F. Place the basket in the air fryer and bake for 8-10 minutes, or until the cheese is melted and the crust is crispy.
3. Remove the pizza from the air fryer and let it cool for a few minutes before slicing and serving.

Potato and Kale Nuggets

SERVINGS
6

TIME
20 min

DIFFICULTY
Easy

INGREDIENTS

- 1 block of firm tofu, drained and cut into 1 to 1.25 inch cubes.
- 2 tbsp olive oil.
- 3 cloves garlic, minced.
- 1 tsp dried oregano.
- 2 tbsp freshly squeezed lemon juice.
- Salt and pepper to taste.

DIRECTIONS

1. Mix together the grated potatoes, chopped kale, grated onion, minced garlic, eggs, flour, breadcrumbs, salt, pepper, and any optional seasonings in a large bowl.
2. Shape the mixture into small nuggets.
3. Preheat your air fryer to 400°F. Place the nuggets in a single layer in the air fryer basket, making sure they are not crowded.
4. Fry for 10-15 minutes, flipping the nuggets halfway through, until they are golden and crispy.
5. Serve the potato and kale nuggets warm. Enjoy!

Tamarind Glazed Sweet Potatoes

SERVINGS	TIME	DIFFICULTY
2	20 min	Easy

INGREDIENTS

- 4 medium sweet potatoes. Peel and cut them into 1/2-inch rounds.
- 1 tablespoon honey.
- 1 teaspoon grated ginger.
- 2 tablespoons tamarind paste.
- 1 tablespoon rice vinegar.
- 1 tablespoon soy sauce.
- 1 clove garlic, minced.
- Salt and pepper to taste.
- Cooking spray.

DIRECTIONS

1. Mix together the tamarind paste, honey, soy sauce, rice vinegar, ginger, garlic, salt, and pepper in a small saucepan, cook over medium heat until it has thickened, about 5-6 minutes.
2. Preheat your air fryer to 400°F. Lightly spray the air fryer basket with cooking spray.
3. Place the sweet potato rounds in a single layer in the air fryer basket. Fry for 10-12 minutes, flipping the sweet potatoes halfway through, until they are tender and slightly crispy.
4. Brush the glaze over the sweet potatoes and return them to the air fryer for another 2-3 minutes, or until the glaze has caramelized. Serve hot.

Air Fry Dumplings

SERVINGS 6 | **TIME** 20 min | **DIFFICULTY** Easy

INGREDIENTS

- 1 package of dumplings (frozen or fresh).
- Optional dipping sauce (such as soy sauce or vinegar)
- Cooking spray.

DIRECTIONS

1. Lightly spray the air fryer basket with cooking spray.
2. Preheat your air fryer to 400°F. Place the dumplings in a single layer in the air fryer basket, making sure they are not crowded.
3. Fry for 10-12 minutes, flipping the dumplings halfway through, until they are golden and crispy on the outside.
4. Serve the dumplings with your favorite dipping sauce.

Note: If you are using frozen dumplings, you may need to increase the cooking time by a few minutes to fully cook the inside.

Baked Potato With Toppings

SERVINGS 4 | **TIME** 25 min | **DIFFICULTY** Easy

INGREDIENTS

- 4 medium russet potatoes, washed and dried
- Optional toppings: shredded cheese, sour cream, chives, etc.
- Salt.

DIRECTIONS

1. Pierce the potatoes several times with a fork.
2. Preheat your air fryer to 400°F. Place the potatoes in the air fryer basket and cook for 20-25 minutes, flipping the potatoes halfway through, until they are soft and tender.
3. Remove the potatoes from the air fryer and cut a slit in the top of each one.
4. Season the potatoes with salt, and then add your desired toppings.
5. Return the potatoes to the air fryer and cook for an additional 5-10 minutes, until the cheese is melted and the toppings are hot.
6. Serve the baked potatoes hot!

Stuffed Eggplant

SERVINGS
4

TIME
15 min

DIFFICULTY
Easy

INGREDIENTS

- 1 cup cooked rice.
- 2 medium eggplants.
- 1 cup shredded mozzarella cheese.
- 1 tbsp olive oil.
- 1 onion, diced.
- 2 cloves garlic, minced.
- 1 can diced tomatoes.
- 1 tsp dried basil.
- 1 tsp dried oregano.
- Salt and pepper to taste.

DIRECTIONS

1. Cut the eggplants in half lengthwise and scoop out the flesh, leaving a 1/4-inch border. Dice the scooped-out eggplant flesh and set aside.
2. In a large pan, heat the olive oil over medium heat. Add the onion and garlic and cook until soft, about 4-5 minutes. Add the diced eggplant to the skillet and cook for an additional 5 minutes, until softened.
3. Stir in the cooked rice, diced tomatoes, basil, oregano, salt, and pepper. Cook until heated through.
4. Fill the eggplant halves with the rice mixture and top each one with 1/4 cup of shredded mozzarella cheese.
5. Preheat your air fryer to 400°F. Place the stuffed eggplant halves in the air fryer basket and cook for 10-15 minutes, until the cheese is melted and bubbly.
6. Serve the stuffed eggplant hot, enjoy!

Garlic-Lemon Tofu

SERVINGS
2

TIME
20 min

DIFFICULTY
Easy

INGREDIENTS

- 1 block of firm tofu, drained and cut into 1 to 1.25 inch cubes.
- 2 tbsp olive oil.
- 3 cloves garlic, minced.
- 1 tsp dried oregano.
- 2 tbsp freshly squeezed lemon juice.
- Salt and pepper to taste.

DIRECTIONS

1. Mix together the tofu cubes, garlic, olive oil, lemon juice, oregano, salt, and pepper in a large bowl.
2. Place the tofu in a single layer in the air fryer basket preheated to 400°F, making sure they are not crowded. Fry for 10-15 minutes, flipping the tofu halfway through, until it is golden and crispy.
3. Serve the garlic-lemon tofu as a side dish or as a protein addition to salads or grain bowls.

Crispy and Salty Tofu

SERVINGS
14

TIME
20 min

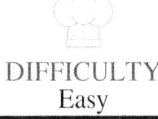
DIFFICULTY
Easy

INGREDIENTS

- 14 ounces firm tofu. Cut into 1/2-inch cubes.
- 2 tablespoons cornstarch.
- 1/2 teaspoon black pepper.
- 1 teaspoon salt.
- Cooking spray.

DIRECTIONS

1. In a shallow dish, mix together the cornstarch, salt, and pepper. Dredge each tofu cube in the cornstarch mixture.
2. Preheat your air fryer to 400°F. Lightly spray the air fryer basket with cooking spray.
3. Place the coated tofu cubes in a single layer in the air fryer basket, making sure they are not crowded.
4. Fry for 10-12 minutes, flipping the tofu halfway through, until it is golden and crispy on the outside.
5. Serve. Enjoy!

Panko Tofu

SERVINGS	TIME	DIFFICULTY
2	20 min	Easy

INGREDIENTS

- 2 eggs, beaten.
- 1 block of firm tofu, drained and cut into 1 to 1.25-inch cubes.
- 1/2 cup all-purpose flour.
- 1 cup panko breadcrumbs.
- Salt and pepper to taste.
- Optional seasonings (e.g., paprika, garlic powder, onion powder)

DIRECTIONS

1. In a shallow dish, mix together the panko breadcrumbs, salt, pepper, flour and any optional seasonings.
2. In another shallow dish, beat the eggs.
3. Dip each tofu cube into the beaten eggs, then coat in the panko mixture.
4. Preheat your air fryer to 400°F. Place the coated tofu cubes in a single layer in the air fryer basket, making sure they are not crowded.
5. Fry for 10-15 minutes, flipping the tofu halfway through, until it is golden and crispy.
6. Serve the panko tofu as a main dish or as a protein addition to salads or grain bowls.

Vegan Sushi Rolls

SERVINGS
2

TIME
20 min

DIFFICULTY
Easy

INGREDIENTS

- 200g pasta.
- 1 red bell pepper, sliced.
- 1 yellow bell pepper, sliced.
- 1 red onion, sliced.
- 1 cup cherry tomatoes, halved.
- 1 garlic, minced.
- 1 tsp dried basil.
- 1/4 cup freshly grated parmesan cheese.
- 2 tbsp freshly squeezed lemon juice.
- 2 tbsp balsamic vinegar.
- 2 tbsp olive oil.
- Salt and pepper to taste..

Vegan Sushi Rolls
(CONTINUES)

DIRECTIONS

1. Cook the sushi rice according to package instructions. Let the rice cool to room temperature.
2. In a small saucepan, heat the rice vinegar, sugar, and salt over medium heat until the sugar is dissolved. Slowly pour the vinegar mixture over the rice, stirring gently to combine.
3. To assemble the rolls, place a sheet of nori seaweed on a flat surface, shiny side down. Spread a thin layer of the rice over the nori, leaving a 1-inch border at the top. Arrange the avocado, carrot, cucumber, and red bell pepper in a line on top of the rice, close to the bottom border.
4. Roll the sushi tightly, using the bottom border of rice to help seal the roll. Cut the sushi rolls into 8 pieces.
5. Put the sushi rolls in the air fryer basket, making sure they are not crowded. Fry at 400°F for 5-7 minutes, or until the rolls are crispy and golden.
6. Serve with soy sauce and pickled ginger. Enjoy!

Crispy Green Tomatoes

SERVINGS	TIME	DIFFICULTY
12	20 min	Easy

INGREDIENTS

- 2 eggs.
- 1 cup all-purpose flour.
- 4 medium green tomatoes.
- 1 cup breadcrumbs.
- Salt and pepper to taste.
- Optional seasonings (e.g., paprika, garlic powder, onion powder).
- Cooking spray.

DIRECTIONS

1. Slice the green tomatoes into 1/2-inch rounds.
2. Mix together the flour, salt, pepper, and any optional seasonings in a shallow dish.
3. In second shallow dish, beat the eggs.
4. In a third shallow dish, mix together the breadcrumbs.
5. Dredge each tomato slice in the flour mixture, then dip it into the beaten eggs, and finally coat it in the breadcrumbs.
6. Preheat your air fryer to 400°F. Lightly spray the air fryer basket with cooking spray. Place the coated tomato slices in a single layer in the air fryer basket, making sure they are not crowded.
7. Fry for 10-12 minutes, flipping the slices halfway through, until they are golden and crispy on the outside. Serve.

Lemon Lentils and Fried Onion

SERVINGS 8 | **TIME** 20 min | **DIFFICULTY** Easy

INGREDIENTS

- 1 cup green lentils.
- 4 cups water.
- 1 onion, thinly sliced.
- 2 tablespoons all-purpose flour.
- 2 tablespoons cornstarch.
- 1/4 cup lemon juice.
- 2 tablespoons olive oil.
- 2 cloves garlic, minced.
- 1/2 teaspoon dried thyme.
- 1/2 teaspoon dried basil.
- 1/2 teaspoon paprika.
- Salt and pepper to taste.
- Cooking spray.

DIRECTIONS

1. Rinse the lentils then cook for 25-30 minutes or until they are tender.
2. Mix together the flour, cornstarch, salt, and pepper in a shallow dish, dip the sliced onion into the flour mixture, making sure it is well coated.
3. Lightly spray oil in the basket of an air fryer preheated to 380 degrees F. Place the coated onion slices in a single layer in the air fryer basket, fry for 10-12 minutes, flipping the onion slices halfway through, until they are golden and crispy.
4. In a saucepan, mix together the lemon juice, olive oil, garlic, thyme, basil, and paprika. Cook the mixture over medium heat until the garlic is fragrant, about 2-3 minutes. Drain the lentils and place them in a serving dish. Pour the lemon mixture over the lentils and stir to combine.
5. Serve the lemon lentils topped with the fried onion.

Roasted Kale Chips

SERVINGS
2

TIME
20 min

DIFFICULTY
Easy

INGREDIENTS

- 1 lb Sweet Potatoes.
- 2 TB Olive Oil.
- 2 Cups Cold Water.
- Salt or Seasoning Blend.

DIRECTIONS

1. Rinse kale Cut kale into approximately 2" pieces. Then rub kale with BBQ rub or seasoning of choice.
2. Toss seasoned kale with just enough oil to coat the leaves lightly.
3. Lightly salt kale to taste
4. Put seasoned kale in air fryer basket Place basket in air fryer and cook at 350°F for 5 minutes.
5. Remove the basket and flip the kale ensuring that no pieces are sticking to the basket Replace the basket in the air fryer and cook at 350° for 5 minutes and add salt to taste.

Herbed Pita Chips

SERVINGS
2

TIME
20 min

DIFFICULTY
Easy

INGREDIENTS

- 4 pita bread rounds.
- 1 tsp dried oregano.
- 2 tbsp olive oil.
- 1 tsp garlic powder.
- 1 tsp dried basil.
- Salt and pepper to taste.

DIRECTIONS

1. Cut each pita bread round into 8 wedges.
2. Mix together the pita wedges, olive oil, basil, oregano, garlic powder, salt, and pepper in a large bowl.
3. Preheat the air fryer to 400°F then place the pita wedges in the air fryer basket in a single layer. Fry for 5-7 minutes, or until the pita chips are golden and crispy.
4. Remove the pita chips from the air fryer and serve warm.

Lemony Pear Chips

SERVINGS
2

TIME
20 min

DIFFICULTY
Easy

INGREDIENTS

- 2 ripe pears.
- 1 tbsp sugar.
- 1 lemon, juiced.
- Salt to taste.

DIRECTIONS

1. Slice the pears into thin rounds.
2. Mix together the pear slices, lemon juice, sugar, and salt in a large bowl.
3. Preheat the air fryer to 400°F. Place the pear slices in the air fryer basket in a single layer. Fry for 8-10 minutes, or until the pear slices are crisp and slightly browned.
4. Remove the pear chips from the air fryer and let them cool to room temperature.

Vegan Popcorn

SERVINGS
2

TIME
20 min

DIFFICULTY
Easy

INGREDIENTS

- 1/4 cup popcorn kernels.
- 2 tbsp vegetable oil.
- Salt to taste.

DIRECTIONS

1. Mix together the popcorn kernels and vegetable oil in a small bowl.
2. Preheat the air fryer to 400°F. Pour the popcorn kernel mixture into the air fryer basket. Fry for 4-5 minutes, or until the popping slows down.
3. Remove the popcorn from the air fryer and sprinkle with salt.
4. Serve the popcorn hot and enjoy!

Crunchy Onion Rings

SERVINGS 4
TIME 20 min
DIFFICULTY Easy

INGREDIENTS

- 1 large sweet onion, sliced very thin.
- large bowl of ice water..
- 1 cup self-rising flour.
- 1 teaspoon salt.
- 1/2 teaspoon pepper.
- 1 teaspoon paprika.
- 1/2 teaspoon garlic powder non-stick.
- cooking spray.

DIRECTIONS

1. Soak the onions in the ice water for at least 10 minutes.
2. Mix the flour with salt, pepper, paprika and garlic powder in a large bowl.
3. Remove the onions from the ice water and toss in the seasoned flour. Shake off all excess flour.
4. Place an even row of onions in the basket, do not overcrowd, and spritz with non-stick spray.
5. Put the basket and pan into the air fryer. Set temperature to 400 F degrees and the timer for 7 minutes.
6. Shake several times during the cooking process. Once cooking is complete, remove. Repeat with remaining onions.

Simple Potato Chips

SERVINGS
4

TIME
30 min

DIFFICULTY
Easy

INGREDIENTS

- 4 potatoes, scrubbed, peeled into thin chips, soaked in water for 30 minutes, drained and pat dried.
- 2 teaspoons rosemary, chopped.
- 1 tablespoon olive oil.
- Salt the taste.

DIRECTIONS

1. Mix potato chips with salt and oil in a bowl.
2. Preheat the air fryer at 250 degrees F in 3 minutes.
3. Place them in your air fryer's basket and cook at 330 degrees F for 30 minutes.
4. Divide among plates, sprinkle rosemary all over and serve as a side dish.

Sweet Potato Fries

SERVINGS	TIME	DIFFICULTY
2	20 min	Easy

INGREDIENTS

- 1/2 Bunch of Young Kale Leaves.
- BBQ Rub or Seasoning of Choice.
- Salt.
- Olive Oil.

DIRECTIONS

1. Cut potatoes into 1/2 inch squared slices then put sliced potatoes into cold water. Soak 30 minutes.
2. Remove potatoes from water and pat dry. Toss potatoes with olive oil until lightly coated.
3. Sprinkle salt or seasoning blend on top of potatoes and stir to combine.
4. Put seasoned potatoes in airfryer basket ensuring that they are no more than two layers thick.
5. Put basket in airfryer and cook at 350° F for 12 minutes.
6. Stir fries to ensure that they cook evenly then fry at 350°F for 12 more minutes.

Note: *For crispier fries, cook at 390°F for 10 minutes each time.*

Crunchy Eggplant Fries

SERVINGS: 2
TIME: 20 min
DIFFICULTY: Easy

INGREDIENTS

- 1 large eggplant.
- 2 cups seasoned panko bread crumbs
- 2 tablespoons milk.
- 1 large egg, beaten.
- 1/2 cup shredded Italian cheese blend
- Cooking spray
- Marinara for dipping

DIRECTIONS

1. Peel the eggplant and slice lengthwise into 0.5-inch slices. Then cut them into quarter-inch strips. In a shallow glass, beat egg and milk together.
2. In another bowl, combine panko and cheese.
3. Dip each piece of eggplant in egg mixture then press into panko mixture, coat both sides well.
4. Place an even layer of eggplant in the basket, do not overcrowd, and spritz with non-stick spray. Put the basket and pan into the air fryer and set temperature to 400 F degrees in 5 minutes.
5. Once baking is complete, remove. Repeat with remaining eggplant.
6. Serve warm with marinara sauce for dipping.

Chocolate Cake

Servings: 12   40 minutes

INGREDIENTS

- 1 egg.
- 1 banana, mashed.
- 3/4 cup white flour.
- 3/4 teaspoon pumpkin pie spice.
- 3/4 cup whole wheat flour.
- 1 teaspoon baking soda.
- 8 ounces canned pumpkin puree.
- 3/4 cup sugar.
- 2/3 cup chocolate chips.
- 1/2 teaspoon baking powder.
- 1/2 teaspoon vanilla extract.
- 2 tablespoons canola oil.
- 1/2 cup Greek yogurt.
- Cooking spray.

DIRECTIONS

1. Mix white flour with whole wheat flour, salt, baking soda and powder and pumpkin spice in a bowl and stir.
2. In another bowl, mix sugar with oil, banana, yogurt, pumpkin puree, vanilla and egg and stir using a mixer.
3. Combine the 2 mixtures, add chocolate chips, stir, pour this into a greased Bundt pan. (Note to choose the Bundt pan that is the right size for the air fryer)
4. Introduce in your air fryer and bake at 330 degrees F for 30 minutes.
5. Leave the cake to cool down, before cutting and serving it.

Coffee Cheesecakes

🍴 Servings: 6   🕐 30 minutes

INGREDIENTS

The cheesecakes:
- 3 eggs.
- 2 tablespoons butter.
- 1/3 cup sugar.
- 8 ounces cream cheese.
- 3 tablespoons coffee.
- 1 tablespoon caramel syrup.

The frosting:
- 3 tablespoons butter.
- 2 tablespoons sugar.
- 3 tablespoons caramel syrup.
- 8 ounces mascarpone cheese, soft.

DIRECTIONS

1. Mix cream cheese with eggs, 2 tablespoons butter, coffee, 1 tablespoon caramel syrup and 1/3 cup sugar in your blender and pulse well.
2. Pour the above mixture into a cake pan that fits in your air fryer.
3. Introduce in the fryer and bake at 320 degrees F and bake for 20 minutes.
4. Leave aside to cool down and then put it in the fridge for 3 hours.
5. Meanwhile, mix 3 tablespoons butter with 3 tablespoons caramel syrup, 2 tablespoons sugar and mascarpone in a bowl, blend well, spoon this over cheesecakes and serve them.

Lemon Pound Cake

🍴 Servings: 1 Mini Loaf 🕐 40 minutes

INGREDIENTS

- 1 large egg.
- 1 cup all-purpose flour.
- 1 teaspoon baking powder.
- 1/4 teaspoon salt.
- 1 lemon, zested.
- 6 tablespoons unsalted butter, softened.
- 1/4 cup buttermilk.
- 1/4 cup granulated sugar.
- 1 tablespoon fresh lemon juice.

<u>Items needed:</u> 1 mini loaf pan, greased

DIRECTIONS

1. Mix together the flour, baking powder, and salt in a bowl.
2. Beat the softened butter with an electric mixer for 3 minutes or until light and fluffy.
3. Add the sugar into the whipped butter, mix well in 1 minute.
4. Add the flour mixture into the butter mix well until fully incorporated.
5. Mix the egg, lemon juice, and lemon zest. Mix on low speed until fully incorporated. Pour in the buttermilk slowly while mixing at medium speed.
6. Add the batter to the greased mini loaf pan, filling all the way to the top.
7. Place cake into the preheated air fryer. Bake in 350 F on 35 minutes.
8. Take out and use immediately or serve cold.

Lime Cheesecake

Servings: 12   40 minutes

INGREDIENTS

- 2 tablespoons butter, melted.
- 1/4 cup coconut, shredded.
- 2 teaspoons sugar.
- 4 ounces flour.

The filling:
- 1 pound cream cheese.
- 2 sachets lime jelly.
- Grated Juice form 1 lime.
- Zest from 1 lime,
- 2 cups hot water.

DIRECTIONS

1. Mix coconut with flour, butter and sugar in a bowl, stir well and put this on the bottom of a pan that fits your air fryer.
2. Meanwhile, put the hot water in another bowl, add jelly sachets and stir until it dissolves.
3. Put cream cheese in a bowl, add jelly, lime juice and zest and whisk really well.
4. Add this over the crust, spread, introduce in the air fryer and cook at 300 degrees F for 4 minutes.
5. Keep in the fridge for 4 hours before servin.

Sponge Cake

Servings: 12   40 minutes

INGREDIENTS

- 1.5 cup milk.
- 1.7 cup sugar.
- 3 cups flour.
- 3 teaspoons baking powder.
- 1/2 cup cornstarch.
- 1 teaspoon baking soda.
- 1 cup olive oil.
- 1/4 cup lemon juice.
- 2 teaspoons vanilla extract.
- 2 cups water.

DIRECTIONS

1. Mix flour with cornstarch, baking powder, baking soda and sugar in a bowl and whisk well.
2. In second bowl, mix oil with milk, water, lemon juice and vanilla and whisk.
3. Combine the two mixtures, stir, pour in a greased baking dish that fits your air fryer.
4. Introduce in the fryer and bake at 350 degrees F for 20 minutes.
5. Leave cake to cool down, cut and serve.

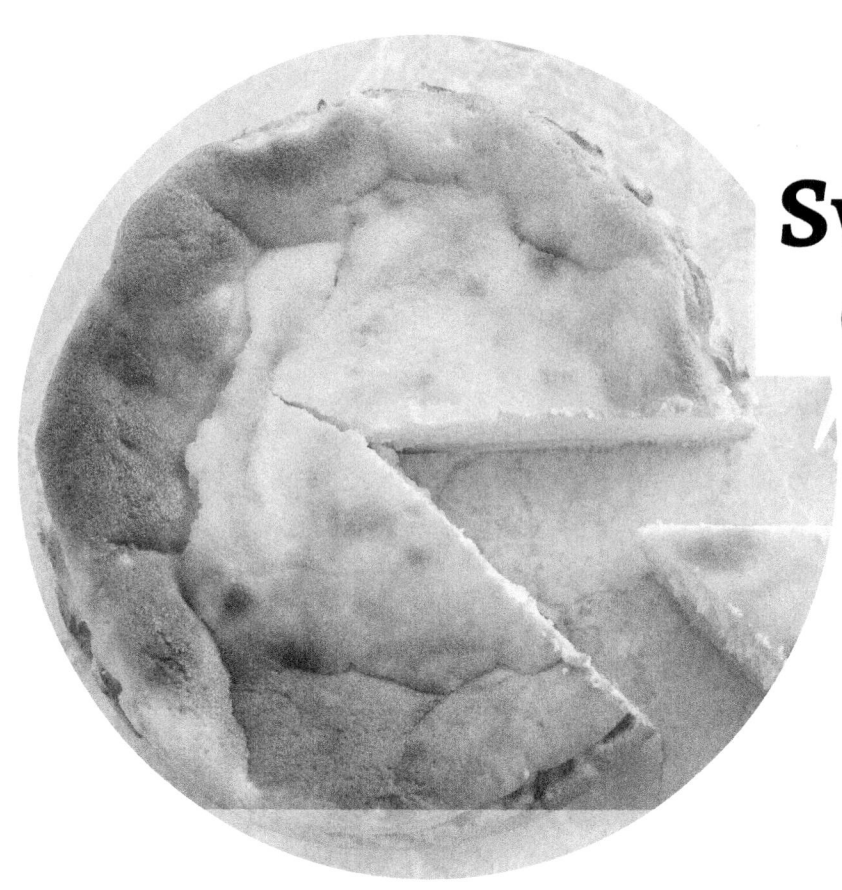

Sweet Potato Cheesecake

🍴 Servings: 4   🕒 15 minutes

INGREDIENTS

- 3/4 cup milk.
- 4 tablespoons butter, melted.
- 8 ounces cream cheese, soft.
- 6 ounces mascarpone, soft.
- 1 teaspoon vanilla extract.
- 2/3 cup graham crackers, crumbled.
- 1/4 teaspoons cinnamon powder.
- 2/3 cup sweet potato puree.

DIRECTIONS

1. Mix butter with crumbled crackers in a bowl, stir well, press on the bottom of a cake pan that fits your air fryer and keep in the fridge for now.
2. In second bowl, mix cream cheese with mascarpone, sweet potato, milk, puree, cinnamon and vanilla and whisk really well.
3. Take the pie crust out of the fridge, spread this over crust, introduce in your air fryer, cook at 300 degrees F for 5 minutes.
4. Keep in the fridge for a few hours before serving.

Carrot Cake

Servings: 6   50 minutes

INGREDIENTS

- 1 egg
- 5 ounces flour.
- ½ teaspoon cinnamon powder
- ½ teaspoon baking soda
- ¾ teaspoon baking powder
- ½ teaspoon allspice
- ¼ cup pineapple juice
- ¼ teaspoon nutmeg, ground
- 1/3 cup carrots, grated
- 3 tablespoons yogurt
- ½ cup sugar
- 1/3 cup coconut flakes, shredded
- 4 tablespoons sunflower oil
- 1/3 cup pecans, toasted and chopped
- Cooking spray.

DIRECTIONS

1. Mix flour with baking soda and powder, salt, allspice, cinnamon and nutmeg in a bowl and stir.
2. In another bowl, mix egg with yogurt, sugar, pineapple juice, oil, carrots, pecans and coconut flakes and stir well.
3. Combine the two mixtures and stir well, pour this into a spring form pan that fits your air fryer which you've greased with cooking spray,
4. Put to your air fryer and bake on 320 degrees F for 40-45 minutes.
5. Leave cake to cool down, then cut and serve it.

Cardamom Cakes

🍴 Servings: 4   🕐 15 minutes

INGREDIENTS

- 2 cups All-purpose flour.
- 1.5 cup milk.
- 1 tbsp cardamom powder.
- 1/2 tsp baking powder.
- 1/2 tsp baking soda.
- 2 tbsp butter.
- 2 tbsp sugar.
- Muffin cups.

DIRECTIONS

1. In a bowl, mix the dry ingredients well to get a acrumbly mixture.
2. In another bowl, mix well the baking soda and the vinegar to the milk, add this milk to the mixture in step 1 and create a batter. Pour into the muffin cups.
3. Preheat the fryer to 300 F for 4 minutes. Put the muffin cups in the basket and bake for 15 minutes.
4. Remove the cups and serve hot.

Poppyseed Cake

🍴 Servings: 6   🕐 40 minutes

INGREDIENTS

- 2 eggs, whisked.
- 3/4 cup sugar.
- 1.25 cups flour.
- 2 teaspoons lime zest, grated.
- 1 teaspoon baking powder.
- 1 tablespoon orange zest, grated.
- 1/2 cup butter, soft
- 1/2 teaspoon vanilla extract.
- 2 tablespoons poppy seeds.
- 1 cup milk.

For the cream:
- 1 cup sugar.
- 4 egg yolks.
- 3 tablespoons butter, melted.
- 1/2 cup passion fruit puree.

DIRECTIONS

1. Mix flour with baking powder, 3/4 cup sugar, orange zest and lime zest in a bowl, and stir.
2. Add 1/2 cup butter, poppy seeds, eggs, vanilla and milk, stir using your mixer, pour into a cake pan that fits your air fryer and bake at 350 degrees F for about 30 minutes.
3. Meanwhile, heat up a pan with 3 tablespoons butter over medium heat, add sugar and stir until it dissolves. Add passion fruit puree and egg yolks gradually and whisk really well. Take off heat.
4. Take cake out of the fryer, cool it down a bit and cut into halves horizontally.
5. Spread 1/4 of passion fruit cream over one half, top with the other cake half and spread 1/4 of the cream on top.
6. Serve cold.

Tangerine Cake

Servings: 8 | 20 minutes

INGREDIENTS

- 1/2 cup milk.
- 3/4 cup sugar.
- 1/2 teaspoon vanilla extract.
- 2 cups flour.
- 1/4 cup olive oil.
- 1 teaspoon cider vinegar.
- Juice and zest from 1 tangerine.
- Juice and zest from 2 lemons.
- Tangerine segments, for serving.

DIRECTIONS

1. Mix flour with sugar in a bowl and stir.
2. In second bowl, mix oil with milk, vanilla extract, vinegar, lemon juice and zest and tangerine zest and whisk very well.
3. Combine the 2 mixtures in 2 bowls together, stir well, pour this into a cake pan that fits your air fryer, introduce in the fryer and cook at 360 degrees F for 20 minutes.
4. Serve right away with tangerine segments on top.

Triple Berry Turnovers

Servings: 6   40 minutes

INGREDIENTS

- 1/2 cup mixed berries, chopped.
- 1/2 cup berry jam.
- 1 pkg (14 oz) refrigerator rolled pie pastry.
- 1 egg.
- 1/2 cup icing sugar.
- 1 tbsp milk.

DIRECTIONS

1. Mix together berries and jam. Let stand for 8 minutes.
2. On lightly floured surface, roll out pie pastry; using 5-inch ring mold or round cookie cutter, cut out 6 rounds.
3. Whisk egg with 2 tsp water; brush over one-half of the edges of pastry rounds. Spread 1 tbsp berry jam over egg-washed half of pastry rounds, leaving border; fold remaining pastry over jam and press edges firmly with fork to seal. Pierce top of tarts with fork to make steam vents. Warm up remaining berry jam.
4. Brush top of tarts with remaining egg wash. Place tarts in bowl of air-fryer. Bake at 300 F in 12 - 15 minutes or until golden and flaky. Let cool completely.
5. Stir icing sugar with milk until smooth. Drizzle turnovers with icing and top with remaining berry jam.

Tip: Try peaches and peach jam, apples and apple butter or cherries and cherry jam.

Strawberry Cupcakes

INGREDIENTS

- 100g Butter.
- 100g Caster Sugar.
- 2 Medium Eggs.
- 100g Self Raising Flour .
- 1/2 Tsp Vanilla Essence.
- 50g Butter.
- 100g Icing Sugar.
- 1/2 Tsp Pink Food Colouring.
- 1 Tbsp Whipped Cream.
- 1/4 Cup Fresh.
- Strawberries (blended)

Servings: 10   25 minutes

DIRECTIONS

1. Mix cream the butter and sugar in a large mixing bowl until the mixture is light and fluffy.
2. Add the vanilla essence and beat in the eggs one at a time. After adding each egg add a little of the flour. Gently fold in the rest of the flour.
3. Put them to little bun cases so that they are 1/3. Then put them in a preheated air fryer for 5 minutes and then bake for 8 minutes at 170 degrees Celsius.
4. While the cupcakes are cooking make the topping. Cream the butter and gradually add the icing sugar until you have a creamy mixture. Add the food colouring, whipped cream and blended strawberries and mix well
5. Once the cupcakes are cooked, using a piping bag add your topping to them doing circular motions so that you have that lovely cupcake look and serve.

Mini Chocolate Peanut Butter Cupcakes

Servings: 40   45 minutes

INGREDIENTS

- 1 cup peanut butter.
- 1/4 cup water, boiling.
- Peanut Butter Frosting.
- 1 stick unsalted butter, softened.
- 2 cups confectioners sugar.
- 1 tbsp whole milk
- Garnish
- Chocolate pearls
- 1 large egg.
- 1/2 cup whole milk.
- 1 cup sugar.
- 1 tsp baking powder.
- 1/4 cup vegetable oil.
- 1.5 tsp vanilla extract.
- 2/3 cup flour.
- 1/3 cup cocoa.
- 1/2 tsp baking soda.
- 1/2 tsp salt.

DIRECTIONS

1. Mix the egg, 1/2 cup milk, vegetable oil, and vanilla in a bowl and whisk to combine.
2. Combine the flour, sugar, cocoa, baking powder, baking soda, and salt with the egg mixture and stir.
3. Slowly add the boiling water to the mixture and whisk the mixture well.
4. Pour the batter into mini aluminum cupcake liners until about two-thirds of each cupcake liner is filled.
5. Place the cake pans in the preheated air fryer. Bake on 15-min in 350° F.
6. In that time, combine the peanut butter and the butter in a bowl. Add the confectioners' sugar and 1 tbsp. milk slowly until the frosting is creamy.
7. Let the cupcakes cool for 30 mins.
8. Top the cupcakes with the frosting and the chocolate pearls and serve.

Maple Cupcakes

🍴 Servings: 4   🕐 30 minutes

INGREDIENTS

- 4 eggs.
- 4 tablespoons butter.
- 2 teaspoons cinnamon powder.
- 1/2 cup pure applesauce.
- 1/2 apple, cored and chopped.
- 1 teaspoon vanilla extract.
- 3/4 cup white flour.
- 4 teaspoons maple syrup.
- 1/2 teaspoon baking powder.

DIRECTIONS

1. Heat up a pan with the butter over medium heat, add applesauce, vanilla, eggs and maple syrup, stir, take off heat and leave aside to cool down.
2. Add flour, cinnamon, baking powder and apples, whisk.
3. Pour in a cupcake pan, introduce in your air fryer at 360 degrees F and bake for 20 minutes.
4. Leave cupcakes them to cool down, transfer to a platter and serve them.

Pumpkin Cupcakes

🍴 Servings: 12   🕐 30 minutes

INGREDIENTS

- 2 large eggs.
- 1 cup all-purpose flour.
- 2 teaspoons pumpkin pie spice.
- 1/2 teaspoon baking powder.
- 1/2 cup sugar.
- 1/4 teaspoon kosher salt.
- 1 stick unsalted butter, room temperature.
- 1/2 cup pumpkin puree.
- 1.5 teaspoon vanilla extract.

DIRECTIONS

1. Sift together the flour, pie spice, baking powder and salt, set aside.
2. With a hand or stand mixer, cream the sugar and butter together until light and fluffy, about 3-4 minutes. Add the pumpkin puree, vanilla and eggs, and mix until smooth and creamy. Slowly add the dry ingredients, mixing until incorporated.
3. Line each silicone muffin cup with a parchment cupcake liner. Fill each cupcake liner 2/3 of the way.
4. Put the cake cups in the air fryer basket. Set temperature to 350 F degrees in 12 minutes.
5. To check for doneness, insert a toothpick in the center of one cupcake. If it comes out clean, it is cooked through.
6. Remove cupcakes to a rack to cool and serve. Cover with Maple Cream Cheese Icing, and sprinkle with brown sugar, if desired.

Black Tea Cake

Servings: 12 **40 minutes**

INGREDIENTS

- 6 tablespoons black tea powder.
- 2 cups milk.
- 1/2 cup butter.
- 2 cups sugar.
- 4 eggs.
- 2 teaspoons vanilla extract.
- 1/2 cup olive oil.
- 3.5 cups flour.
- 1 teaspoon baking soda.
- 3 teaspoons baking powder

For the cream:
- 6 tablespoons honey.
- 4 cups sugar.
- 1 cup butter, soft.

DIRECTIONS

1. Put the milk in a pot, heat up over low heat, add tea, stir well, take off heat and leave aside to cool down.
2. Mix 1/2 cup butter with 2 cups sugar, eggs, vegetable oil, vanilla extract, baking powder, baking soda and 3.5 cups flour in a bowl and stir everything really well.
3. Pour this mixture into 2 greased round pans, introduce each in the fryer at 330 degrees F and bake for 25 minutes.
4. Mix 1 cup butter with honey and 4 cups sugar in another bowl and stir really well.
5. Arrange one cake on a platter, spread the cream all over, top with the other cake and keep in the fridge until you serve it.

Cranberry Cakes

Servings: 4   25 minutes

INGREDIENTS

- 1.5 cup milk.
- 2 cups All-purpose flour.
- 2 tbsp butter.
- 1/2 tsp baking powder.
- 1/2 tsp baking soda.
- 2 tsp vinegar.
- 2 tbsp sugar.
- 2 cups grated cranberries Muffin cups

DIRECTIONS

1. Mix well flour, sugar, butter, baking powder and grated cranberries together until to get acrumbly mixture.
2. Add the baking soda and the vinegar to the milk and mix continuously. Add this milk to the mixture in step 1 and create a batter, which you will need to transfer to the muffin cups.
3. Preheat the fryer to 330 F for 4 minutes. You will need to place the muffin cups in the basket and cover it. Bake the muffins for 15 minutes and check whether or not the muffins are cooked using a toothpick.
4. Remove the cups and serve hot.

Chocolate Muffins

Servings: 12   25 minutes

INGREDIENTS

- 2 Medium Eggs
- 100g Butter
- 200g Self Raising
- 225 Caster Sugar
- 1/2 Tsp Vanilla Essence
- 25g Cocoa Powder
- 75g Milk Chocolate
- 5 Tbsp Milk Water

DIRECTIONS

1. Mix the flour, sugar and cocoa in a large mixing bowl. Rub in the butter until have a breadcrumbs consistency.
2. In second bowl, crack the eggs, add the milk and mix well. Add the egg/milk mixture into the large mixing bowl and mix well.
3. Add the vanilla essence, mix well and then add a little water if it is too thick. You have something that resembles a bun mix.
4. Using a rolling pin bash your milk chocolate in a sandwich bag until they are a mix of sizes. Add it to the bowl and mix again for the last time.
5. Spoon into little bun cases and put the muffins into the preheated air fryer. Bake for 9 minutes on 180c followed by 6 minutes on 160c. And serve.

Blueberry Muffins

🍴 Servings: 6　🕐 45 minutes

INGREDIENTS

- 275g Egg Whites.
- 75g Whey/Casein Blend Vanilla Protein Powder.
- 100g Frozen Blueberries
- 30g Blueberry Pastry Protein Cookie Butter Powder.
- 30g All Purpose Flour.
- 10g Baking Powder.
- 20g Coconut Flour.
- 10g Zero Cal Sweetener of your choice.
- 275g Plain Nonfat Greek Yogurt.
- 100g Unsweetened Apple Sauce.

DIRECTIONS

1. Mix well all the dry ingredients together in a bowl to avoid clumping, then add in your wet ingredients and mix some more. Don't any chunks or clumps. When everything's mixed together, let the batter sit for 15-20 minutes to thicken up.
2. Mix frozen blueberries with the batter, then spray silicon jump muffin molds with nonstick cooking spray. Evenly pour the batter into 6 molds. Be sure to leave enough space between them get don't oddly shaped muffins.
3. Baking the muffins at 250 degrees F for 32-35 minutes. When done, let them cool in their molds for 10-15 minutes, then serve.

Chocolate Chip Muffins

🍴 Servings: 8   🕒 25 minutes

INGREDIENTS

- 1 cup all-purpose flour
- 1/4 cup granulated sugar.
- 1/2 teaspoon vanilla extract.
- 1/2 cup coconut milk or soy milk.
- 3 tablespoons liquidated coconut oil.
- 1/4 teaspoon salt
- 1 teaspoon baking powder
- 2 tablespoons cocoa powder
- 1/4 teaspoon baking soda
- 1/2 cup dark chocolate chips
- 1/4 cup pistachios, cracked (optional)
- Cooking spray
- Muffin pan or baking cups

DIRECTIONS

1. In a bowl, mix sugar, coconut/soy milk, coconut oil, and vanilla extractthen set aside.
2. In a second bowl, mix together flour, cocoa powder, baking powder, baking soda, and salt.
3. Mix the dry ingredients into the wet ingredients gradually, until smooth. Then fold in chocolate chips and pistachios.
4. Preheat the Air Fryer for 300°F in 4 mins.
5. Grease muffin cups with cooking spray and pour in batter until cups are 3/4 full.
6. Put the muffins into the preheated air fryer. Bake muffin for 300°F in 15 minutes. Then take out, let cool and serve.

Oats Muffins

🍴 Servings: 6　🕐 18 minutes

DIRECTIONS

1. Mix the dry ingredients together to get a acrumbly mixture.
2. Divide the milk into two equal parts, then add one to the baking soda and the other to the vinegar.
3. Mix both milk mixtures together and wait until the milk starts to foam. Add this mixture to the crumb mixture and start whisking the ingredients at a high speed.
4. Once you have a smooth batter, pour the mixture into the muffin cups. Preheat the fryer to 300 degrees F for 5 minutes. Then place the muffin cups in the basket and bake at 320 degrees F for 15 minutes Remove and serve hot.

INGREDIENTS

- 2 cups All-purpose flour.
- 1.5 cup milk.
- 1/2 tsp baking powder.
- 1/2 tsp baking soda
- 2 tbsp butter.
- 1 cup sugar.
- 3 tsp vinegar.
- 1 cup oats.
- 1/2 tsp vanilla essence.
- Muffin cups or butter paper cups.

Simple Donuts

 Servings: 6   25 minutes

INGREDIENTS

- 4 tablespoons butter, soft.
- 1/2 cup sour cream.
- 1.5 teaspoon baking powder.
- 2 egg yolks.
- 2.25 cups white flour.
- 1 teaspoon cinnamon powder.
- 1/2 cup sugar.
- 1/3 cup caster sugar.

DIRECTIONS

1. Mix 2 tablespoons of butter with simple sugar and egg yolks and beat well in a bowl.
2. Add half of the sour cream to the bowl and stir.
3. In another bowls, mix flour with baking powder, stir. Then add the egg mixture in step 1 and 2 and stir well
4. Stir until you obtain a dough, transfer it to a floured working surface, roll it out and cut big circles with smaller ones in the middle.
5. Brush doughnuts with the rest of the butter, heat up your air fryer at 360 degrees F in 3 minutes, place doughnuts inside and bake them for 8 minutes.
6. Mix cinnamon with caster sugar in a bowl.
7. Arrange doughnuts on plates and dip them in cinnamon sugar mixture before serving.

Vanilla Mini Donuts

Servings: 27   25 minutes

INGREDIENTS

- 412g Egg Whites
- 75g All Purpose Flour
- 75g Whey/Casein Blend Vanilla Protein Powder
- 15g Baking Powder
- 36g Birthday Cake Batter Protein Cookie Butter Powder
- 30g Coconut Flour
- 15g Zero Cal Sweetener of your choice
- 412g Plain Nonfat Greek Yogurt
- 150g Unsweetened Apple Sauce

DIRECTIONS

1. Add all your dry ingredients into a bowl and mix well to avoid clumping. Then add your wet ingredients and mix until combined.
2. Add mini donut silicone molds to your air fryer and spray with non stick cooking spray.
3. Add your batter to each leaving a little bit from the top because these will rise. Bake for 250 degrees F in 15 minutes, then open the air fryer, flip the other side of the bagel, bake for 5 more minutes at the same temperature.
4. Then add whatever frosting your heart desires on top along with toppings and enjoy!

Everything Bagels

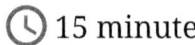
Servings: 6   15 minutes

INGREDIENTS

- 50g Egg Whites
- 45g All Purpose Flour
- 3g Baking Powder
- 8g Coconut Flour
- 3g Everything Bagel Seasoning
- 100g Plain Nonfat Greek Yogurt

DIRECTIONS

1. In a bowl, mix all of your dry ingredients together, then add in your wet ingredients and mix everything together.
2. Spray mini silicone bagel molds with nonstick cooking spray and evenly spread your batter to each.
3. Air fry the bagels at 360 degrees F for 8 minutes, then open the air fryer, flip the other side of the bagel, bake for another 4-6 minutes until golden.
4. When they're done, let the bagels cool on a cooling rack. Don't cut them out right away as they will be super soft in the middle.

Strawberry Donuts

🍴 Servings: 4   🕐 25 minutes

INGREDIENTS

- 8 ounces flour.
- 1 tablespoon brown sugar.
- 1 tablespoon white sugar.
- 1 egg.
- 2.5 tablespoons butter.
- 4 ounces whole milk.
- 1 teaspoon baking powder.

For the strawberry icing:
- 2 tablespoons butter.
- 3.5 ounces icing sugar.
- ½ teaspoon pink coloring.
- ¼ cup strawberries, chopped.
- 1 tablespoon whipped cream.

DIRECTIONS

1. Mix butter, 1 tablespoon brown sugar, 1 tablespoon white sugar and flour in a bowl and stir.
2. In another bowl, mix egg with 1.5 tablespoons butter and milk and stir well.
3. Combine the 2 mixtures, stir, shape donuts from this mix, place them in your air fryer's basket and bake at 360 degrees F for 15-18 minutes.
4. Put 1 tablespoon butter, icing sugar, food coloring, whipped cream and strawberry puree and whisk well.
5. Arrange donuts on a platter and pour the strawberry sauce on top and enjoy.

Coconut Donuts

Servings: 4　　25 minutes

INGREDIENTS

- 1 large egg.
- 1.5 cups all-purpose flour.
- 1/2 cup buttermilk.
- 3 tbsp (45g) unsalted butter, melted.
- 1/2 cup unsweetened shredded coconut.
- 1/2 cup sweetened shredded coconut, for coating.
- 1/2 cup granulated sugar.
- 1 tsp baking powder.
- 1/2 tsp baking soda.
- 1/2 tsp salt.
- 1 tsp vanilla extract.

DIRECTIONS

1. Whisk together flour, unsweetened shredded coconut, sugar, baking powder, baking soda, and salt in a bowl.
2. In another bowl, whisk together the buttermilk, eggs, vanilla extract, and melted butter. Blend dry ingredients into wet ingredients and stir until combined.
3. Scoop the batter into the greased donut pan, filling each pan about 2/3 full. Place them in the air fryer and bake at 360°F for 12-15 minutes.
4. Remove the donuts from the basket and let cool, rolling each donut in a dish of grated coconut to coat. Enjoy !

Coffee Donuts

🍴 Servings: 4   🕐 25 minutes

INGREDIENTS

- 1 large egg.
- 1.5 cups all-purpose flour.
- 1/2 cup buttermilk.
- 3 tbsp (45g) unsalted butter, melted.
- 1/2 cup unsweetened shredded coconut.
- 1/2 cup sweetened shredded coconut, for coating.
- 1/2 cup granulated sugar.
- 1 tsp baking powder.
- 1/2 tsp baking soda.
- 1/2 tsp salt.
- 1 tsp vanilla extract.

DIRECTIONS

1. Mix flour, sugar, baking powder, baking soda and salt in a bowl.
2. In the second bowl, mix the cooled coffee, eggs, vanilla extract, and melted butter. Blend dry ingredients into wet ingredients and stir until combined.
3. Pour the dough into the donut mold. Place the filled mold in the air fryer and bake at 380°F for 10-12 minutes.
4. Remove the donuts from the air fryer and let cool for a few minutes before removing from the pan. Roll each donut in a plate of coffee or cocoa powder for coating. Enjoy !

Lemon Poppyseed Donuts

Servings: 4   25 minutes

INGREDIENTS

- 1 large egg.
- 1.5 cups all-purpose flour.
- 1/2 cup granulated sugar.
- 1/2 cup powdered sugar, for coating.
- 1/2 cup buttermilk.
- 1 tsp baking powder.
- 1/2 tsp baking soda.
- 1/2 tsp salt.
- 3 tbsp unsalted butter, melted.
- 2 tbsp lemon zest.
- 2 tbsp poppy seeds.
- 1 tsp vanilla extract.

DIRECTIONS

1. Mix flour, sugar, baking powder, baking soda and salt in a bowl.
2. In another bowl, whisk together the buttermilk, eggs, vanilla extract, melted butter, lemon zest, and poppy seeds. Mix dry ingredients into wet ingredients and stir until just combined.
3. Pour the dough into the donut mold. Place the filled mold in the air fryer and cook at 380°F for 10-12 minutes.
4. Remove the donuts from the air fryer and let cool for a few minutes before removing from the pan. Roll each donut in the sugar dish to coat. Enjoy !

Simple Cookies

🍴 Servings: 12   🕐 20 minutes

INGREDIENTS

- 1 large egg.
- 1 cup (125g) all-purpose flour.
- 1 tsp vanilla extract.
- 3/4 cup (150g) granulated sugar.
- 1/2 tsp baking powder.
- 1/4 tsp salt.
- 1/2 cup (113g) unsalted butter, room temperature.

DIRECTIONS

1. Mix flour, baking powder and salt in a bowl, set aside.
2. In another bowl, beat the buttercream and sugar until light and fluffy then add the eggs and vanilla extract, beating well. Gradually add the dry ingredients in step 1 to the mix until just combined.
3. Use a spoon or spatula to scoop each spoonful of batter onto a parchment lined plate. Place the dough balls in a single layer in the basket of the preheated air fryer.
4. Bake at 330°F (165°C) for 8-10 minutes or until edges are golden brown
5. Remove the cookies from the air fryer and serve to cool.

Brown Butter Cookies

🍴 Servings: 12   🕐 20 minutes

INGREDIENTS

- 2 eggs, whisked.
- 1.5 cups butter.
- 2 cups brown sugar.
- 2/3 cup pecans, chopped.
- 3 cups flour.
- 1 teaspoon baking soda.
- 2 teaspoons vanilla extract.
- 1/2 teaspoon baking powder.

DIRECTIONS

1. Heat up a pan, add butter and cook over medium heat, stir until it melts, add brown sugar and stir until this dissolves.
2. Mix flour with pecans, vanilla extract, baking powder, baking soda, and eggs in a bowl, and stir well.
3. Add brown butter, stir well and arrange spoonfuls of this mix on a lined baking sheet that fits your air fryer.
4. Introduce in the fryer and cook at 340 degrees F for 10 minutes.
5. Leave cookies to cool down and serve.

Potato Chip Cookies

Servings: 12   20 minutes

INGREDIENTS

- 1 large egg.
- 1.5 cups all-purpose flour.
- 1 tsp baking powder.
- 1/2 tsp baking soda.
- 1/2 tsp salt.
- 1/2 cup unsalted butter, room temperature.
- 1 cup semisweet chocolate chips.
- 1/2 cup granulated sugar.
- 1/2 cup brown sugar.
- 2 cups crushed potato chips.
- 1 tsp vanilla extract.

DIRECTIONS

1. Whisk together flour, baking powder, baking soda and salt in a bowl.
2. In another bowl, beat the buttercream, granulated sugar, and brown sugar until light and fluffy, add the eggs and vanilla extract, and stir.
3. Gradually add in dry ingredients and mix until just combined. Stir in the fries and chocolate chips.
4. Use a spoon to scoop each scoop of dough onto the prepared baking tray, placing them at least 2 inches apart. Place in a preheated air fryer. Bake cookies at 380°F for 12-15 minutes or until edges are golden brown.
5. Remove cookies from oven and let cool before serving.

Honey & Oats Cookie

Servings: 18   25 minutes

INGREDIENTS

- 1 cups flour
- 1 cup all-purpose flour
- 1/2 cup milk
- 1 tsp baking powder
- 1 tbsp liquid glucose
- 2 tbsp powdered sugar
- 1/2 cup oats
- 1 tbsp unsalted butter
- 2 tsp honey

DIRECTIONS

1. In a bowl, mix the dry ingredients together and warm the glucose with a little water. Mix the glucose, honey and the butter to the bowl followed by the milk.
2. Roll the dough using a pin. Create cookies and set them on a prepared baking tray.
3. Preheat the fryer to 300 Fahrenheit for 4 minutes. Then put the baking tray in the basket and bake to 250 Fahrenheit in 15 minutes. Turn the cookies in the tray to ensure that they are cooked uniformly.
4. When the cookies have cooled, store them in an airtight container and serve

Lentils Cookies

🍴 Servings: 36   🕐 25 minutes

INGREDIENTS

- 1 egg.
- 1 cup water.
- 1 cup white flour.
- 1 cup canned lentils, drained and mashed.
- 1 teaspoon baking powder.
- 1 teaspoon cinnamon powder.
- 1 cup whole wheat flour.
- 1/2 teaspoon nutmeg, ground.
- 1 cup butter, soft.
- 1/2 cup white sugar.
- 1/2 cup brown sugar.
- 2 teaspoons almond extract.
- 1 cup raisins.
- 1 cup rolled oats.
- 1 cup coconut, unsweetened and shredde.

DIRECTIONS

1. Mix white and whole wheat flour with salt, cinnamon, baking powder and nutmeg in a bowl and stir.
2. In second bowl, mix butter with white and brown sugar and stir using your kitchen mixer for 2 minutes.
3. Add egg, almond extract, lentils mix, flour mix, oats, raisins and coconut and stir everything well.
4. Scoop tablespoons of dough on a lined baking sheet that fits your air fryer, introduce them in the fryer and cook at 350 degrees F for 18 minutes.
5. Arrange cookies on a serving platter and serve.

Pumpkin Cookies

Servings: 24   25 minutes

INGREDIENTS

- 1/4 cup honey.
- 2.5 cups flour.
- 2 tablespoons butter.
- 1/2 teaspoon baking soda.
- 1 tablespoon flax seed, ground.
- 3 tablespoons water.
- 1/2 cup pumpkin flesh, mashed.
- 1/2 cup dark chocolate chips.
- 1 teaspoon vanilla extract.

DIRECTIONS

1. Mix flax seed with water in a bowl, stir and leave aside for a few minutes.
2. In second bowl, mix flour with salt and baking soda.
3. In a third bowl, mix honey with pumpkin puree, butter, vanilla extract and flaxseed.
4. Combine flour with honey mix and chocolate chips and stir.
5. Scoop 1 tablespoon of cookie dough on a lined baking sheet that fits your air fryer, repeat with the rest of the dough, introduce them in your air fryer and cook at 330 degrees F for 18 minutes.
6. Leave cookies to cool down and serve.

Thin and Crispy
Chocolate Chip Cookies

🍴 Servings: 20   🕐 30 minutes

INGREDIENTS

- 2 large eggs.
- 2 cups chocolate chips.
- 2.25 cups all-purpose flour.
- 1 tsp baking soda.
- 1 tsp salt.
- 1 cup unsalted butter, room temperature.
- 3/4 cup granulated sugar.
- 3/4 cup brown sugar.
- 2 tsp vanilla extract.

DIRECTIONS

1. Mix flour, baking soda and salt in a bowl.
2. In the second bowl, whisk together the buttercream, granulated sugar, and brown sugar until smooth and fluffy. Crack the eggs one at a time, then add the vanilla extract and beat well. Gradually add in dry ingredients and mix until just combined. Add the chocolate chips and stir well.
3. Cover the dough and refrigerate for at least 2 hours or overnight.
4. Use a spoon to scoop each scoop of dough onto the prepared baking tray, placing them at least 2 inches apart (For thin and crispy cookie, be sure to flatten the dough balls). Then place in the preheated air fryer basket. Bake at 380°F for 8-10 minutes or until edges are golden brown
5. Take the cookies out of the oven and let it cool completely before serving.

Malted Chocolate Chip Cookie Bars

Servings: 20 30 minutes

INGREDIENTS

- 2 large eggs.
- 2.25 cups all-purpose flour.
- 2 cups chocolate chips.
- 1 tsp baking powder.
- 1/2 tsp baking soda.
- 1/2 tsp salt.
- 1 cup (226g) unsalted butter, room temperature.
- 3/4 cup (150g) granulated sugar.
- 3/4 cup (150g) brown sugar.
- 1/2 cup malted milk powder.
- 2 tsp vanilla extract.

DIRECTIONS

1. Mix flour, baking powder, baking soda and salt in a bowl.
2. In another bowl, beat the buttercream, granulated sugar, and brown sugar until smooth and creamy, then stir in the eggs, vanilla extract, and malted milk powder. Gradually add in dry ingredients and mix until just combined. Add the chocolate chips and stir well.
3. Spread batter evenly onto greased baking dish, place in preheated air fryer, bake at 350°F for 25-30 minutes or until edges are golden brown.
4. Remove the bars from the air fryer and let them cool, cut the bars into squares and serve.

Lemon Poppy Seed Tea Cookies

🍴 Servings: 20   🕐 30 minutes

INGREDIENTS

- 1 large egg.
- 2 tbsp poppy seeds.
- 2.25 cups all-purpose flour.
- 1 tsp baking powder.
- 1/4 tsp baking soda.
- 1/2 tsp salt.
- 1 cup unsalted butter, room temperature.
- 3/4 cup granulated sugar.
- 1 tsp vanilla extract.
- 1 tbsp grated lemon zest.
- 2 tbsp freshly squeezed lemon juice.

DIRECTIONS

1. Mix flour, baking powder, baking soda and salt in a bowl.
2. In another bowl, beat cream butter and sugar until smooth and fluffy. Crack in the eggs, then stir in the vanilla extract, lemon juice and lemon zest. Gradually add in dry ingredients and mix until just combined. Stir in the poppy seeds.
3. Use a spoon to scoop each scoop of dough onto the prepared baking tray, placing them at least 2 inches apart. Place the tray in the preheated air fryer basket. Bake cookies at 350°F for 8-10 minutes or until edges are golden brown
4. Remove cookies from air fryer and let cool before serving.

Orange Cookies

🍴 Servings: 8   🕐 20 minutes

INGREDIENTS

- 1 egg, whisked.
- 2 cups flour.
- 3/4 cup sugar.
- 1 teaspoon baking powder.
- 1/2 cup butter, soft.
- 1 tablespoon orange zest, grated.
- 1 teaspoon vanilla extract.

For the filling:
- 4 ounces cream cheese, soft.
- 2 cups powdered sugar.
- 1/2 cup butter.

DIRECTIONS

1. Mix cream cheese with 1/2 cup butter and 2 cups powdered sugar in a bowl, stir well using your mixer and leave aside for now.
2. In second bowl, mix flour with baking powder.
3. In another bowl, mix 1/2 cup butter with 3/4 cup sugar, egg, vanilla extract and orange zest and whisk well.
4. Combine flour with orange mix, stir well and scoop 1 tablespoon of the mix on a lined baking sheet that fits your air fryer.
5. Repeat with the rest of the orange batter, introduce in the fryer and cook at 340 degrees F for 12 minutes.
6. Leave cookies to cool down, spread cream filling on half of them top with the other cookies and serve.

Trail Mix Cookies

🍴 Servings: 12 🕐 30 minutes

DIRECTIONS

- 2 large eggs.
- 2.25 cups all-purpose flour.
- 1 tsp baking powder.
- 1/2 tsp baking soda.
- 1/2 tsp salt.
- 1 cup unsalted butter, room temperature.
- 2 cups semisweet chocolate chips.
- 150g chopped nuts (such as almonds, pecans, or walnuts)
- 120g dried fruit (such as raisins, cranberries, or chopped dates)
- 150g rolled oats.
- 150g granulated sugar.
- 150g brown sugar.
- 1 tsp vanilla extract.

INGREDIENTS

1. Mix flour, baking powder, baking soda and salt in a bowl.
2. In another bowl, beat the buttercream, brown sugar, and granulated sugar until light and fluffy. Add eggs, vanilla extract and mix well. Gradually add in dry ingredients and mix until just combined. Add chocolate chips, nuts, dried fruit, and oats to the mixture until evenly distributed.
3. Scoop each scoop of dough onto the prepared baking tray, placing them at least 2 inches apart. Then put in the preheated air fryer.
4. Bake at 380°F for 12-15 minutes or until edges are lightly golden brown.
5. Remove cookies from oven and let cool before serving.

Buttermilk Biscuits

Servings: 4   25 minutes

INGREDIENTS

- 1.25 cup white flour.
- 1 teaspoon sugar.
- ½ cup self-rising flour.
- ¼ teaspoon baking soda.
- ¾ cup buttermilk Maple syrup for serving.
- ½ teaspoon baking powder.
- 4 tablespoons butter, cold and cubed+ 1 tablespoon melted butter.

DIRECTIONS

1. Mix white flour with self-rising flour, baking soda, baking powder and sugar and stir in a bowl.
2. Add cold butter to the bowl and stir well with the above mixture.
3. Add buttermilk, stir until you obtain a dough and transfer to a floured surface.
4. Roll your dough and cut 10 pieces using a round cutter.
5. Arrange biscuits in your air fryer's cake pan, brush them with melted butter and cook at 400 degrees F for 8 minutes.
6. Serve them for breakfast with some maple syrup on top.

Plum and Currant Tart

Servings: 6   45 minutes

INGREDIENTS

For the crumble:
- 3 tablespoons milk.
- 1 cup brown rice flour
- 1/4 cup almond flour.
- 1/4 cup millet flour.
- 1/2 cup cane sugar.
- 10 tablespoons butter, soft.

For the filling:
- 1 cup white currants.
- 1 pound small plums, pitted and halved.
- 1/4 teaspoon ginger powder.
- 2 tablespoons cornstarch.
- 1 teaspoon lime juice.
- 3 tablespoons sugar.
- 1/2 teaspoon vanilla extract.
- 1/2 teaspoon cinnamon powder.

DIRECTIONS

1. Mix brown rice flour with 1/2 cup sugar, millet flour, almond flour, butter and milk in a bowl and stir until you obtain a sand like dough.
2. Reserve 1/4 of the dough, press the rest of the dough into a tart pan that fits your air fryer and keep in the fridge for 30 minutes.
3. Meanwhile, in a bowl, mix plums with currants, 3 tablespoons sugar, cornstarch, vanilla extract, cinnamon, ginger and lime juice and stir well.
4. Pour this over tart crust, crumble reserved dough on top, introduce in your air fryer and cook at 350 degrees F for 35 minutes.
5. Leave tart to cool down and serve.

Blueberry Tarts

Servings: 10   25 minutes

INGREDIENTS

- 2 tbsp powdered sugar
- 1.5 cup plain flour
- 3 tbsp unsalted butter
- 1 tbsp sliced cashew
- 2 cups cold water

For filling:

- 3 tbsp butter
- 1 cup fresh cream
- 1 cup fresh blueberries (Sliced)

DIRECTIONS

1. Mix well the ingredients together to form a crumbly mixture. Knead the mixture with cold milk and wrap it.
2. Roll the dough into two large circles and place the dough in the cake pan and poke the edges of the dough with a fork.
3. Heat the filling ingredients over low heat and pour over the dough in the tin. Then cover pie tin with the second round.
4. Preheat the fryer to 300 Fahrenheit for 4 minutes. Put the tin in the basket and cover it. bake at 300 Fahrenheit in 8 minutes. When the pastry has turned golden brown, you will need to remove the tin and let it cool. Cut into slices and serve with a dollop of cream.

Chocolate Tarts

 Servings: 8   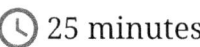 25 minutes

INGREDIENTS

- 1.5 cup plain flour
- 2 cups cold water
- 1/2 cup cocoa powder.
- 2 tbsp powdered sugar
- 3 tbsp unsalted butter
- 1 tbsp sliced cashew

For Truffle filling:
- 3 tbsp butter
- 1.5 melted chocolate
- 1 cup fresh cream

DIRECTIONS

1. Mix the flour, butter, cocoa powder and sugar in a large bowl, . The mixture should resemble breadcrumbs. Knead the dough using the cold milk and wrap it and leave it to cool for 10 minutes.
2. Roll the dough out into the pie and prick the sides of the pie.
3. Mix the ingredients for the filling in another bowl. Make sure that it is a little thick. Add the filling to the pie and cover it with the second round. Put pie into the tin,
4. Preheat the fryer to 300 Fahrenheit for 4 minutes. Put the tin in the basket and cover it. bake at 300 Fahrenheit in 8 minutes. When the pastry has turned golden brown, you will need to remove the tin and let it cool. Cut into slices and serve with a dollop of cream.

Strawberry Jam Tarts

Servings: 9   18 minutes

INGREDIENTS

- Strawberry Jam Water
- 100g Butter
- 225g Plain Flour
- 25g Caster Sugar

DIRECTIONS

1. Mix sugar, flour, and butter in a large bowl. Then rub the fat into the sugar and flour until the mixture resembles breadcrumbs.
2. Add water until you have a soft dough.
3. Grease the bottom and sides of the mini cake pan, pour the batter into the cake pan, top with 2 teaspoons of strawberry (or raspberry) jam, and place in the preheated air fryer. Cook for 10 minutes at 180 degrees Celsius or until the cake is cooked through.
4. Take out the cake to cool and serve.

Lemon Tart

 Servings: 6 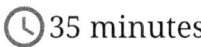 35 minutes

INGREDIENTS

For the crust:
- 2 cups white flour.
- 2 tablespoons sugar.
- 12 tablespoons cold butter.
- 3 tablespoons ice water.
- A pinch of salt.

For the filling:
- 2 eggs, whisked.
- Juice from 2 lemons.
- Zest from 2 lemons, grated.
- 1.25 cup sugar.
- 10 tablespoons melted and chilled butter.

DIRECTIONS

1. Mix 2 cups flour with a pinch of salt and 2 tablespoons sugar in a bowl and whisk.
2. Add 12 tablespoons butter and the water, knead until you obtain a dough, shape a ball, wrap in foil and keep in the fridge for 1 hour.
3. Transfer dough to a floured surface, flatten it, arrange on the bottom of a tart pan, prick with a fork, keep in the fridge for 20 minutes, introduce in your air fryer at 360 degrees F and bake for 15 minutes.
4. In another bowl, mix 1.25 cup sugar with eggs, 10 tablespoons butter, lemon juice and lemon zest and whisk very well.
5. Pour this into pie crust, spread evenly, introduce in the fryer and cook at 360 degrees F for 20 minutes.
6. Cut and serve.

Fruit Tarts

 Servings: 8   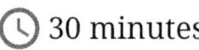 30 minutes

INGREDIENTS

- 3 tbsp unsalted butter
- 1.5 cup plain flour
- 2 cups cold water
- 1/2 cup cocoa powder
- 1 tbsp sliced cashew
- 2 tbsp powdered sugar

For Truffle filling:
- 3 tbsp butter
- 2 cups mixed sliced fruits
- 1 cup fresh cream

DIRECTIONS

1. Mix all the ingredients together using milk into dough that is soft. Roll the dough out and cut into two circles. Press the dough into the pie tins and prick on all sides using a fork.
2. In a bowl, mix the ingredients for the filling. Make sure that it is a little thick. Add the filling to the pie and cover it with the second round.
3. Preheat the fryer to 300 Fahrenheit for 4 minutes. Put the tin in the basket and cover it, bake at 300 Fahrenheit in 8 minutes . When the pastry has turned golden brown, you will need to remove the tin and let it cool. Cut into slices and serve with a dollop of cream.

Banana Bread

SERVINGS
6

TIME
50 min

DIFFICULTY
Medium

INGREDIENTS

- 2 bananas, mashed.
- 3/4 cup sugar.
- 1 teaspoon vanilla extract.
- 1/3 cup butter.
- 1.5 cups flour.
- 1 egg.
- 1 teaspoon baking powder.
- 1/2 teaspoons baking soda.
- 1/3 cup milk.
- 1.5 teaspoons cream of tartar.
- Cooking spray.

DIRECTIONS

1. Mix milk with cream of tartar, sugar, butter, egg, vanilla and bananas In a bowl and stir everything.
2. In second bowl, mix flour with baking powder and baking soda.
3. Combine the 2 above mixtures, stir well, pour this into a cake pan greased with some cooking spray.
4. Introduce in your air fryer and cook at 320 degrees F for 38-40 minutes.
5. Take bread out, leave aside to cool down, slice and serve it.

Banana Nut Bread

SERVINGS
1 Medium Loaf

TIME
50 min

DIFFICULTY
Medium

INGREDIENTS

- 1 egg.
- 1/2 cup sugar.
- 1/4 cup unsalted butter, softened.
- 2 overripe bananas, mashed.
- 1/4 teaspoon vanilla extract.
- 1/2 teaspoon baking soda.
- 1/2 cup chopped walnuts.
- 3/4 cups all-purpose flour
- 1/2 teaspoon salt.
- Cooking spray.

Items needed: 1 mini loaf pan

DIRECTIONS

1. Mix Cream together the butter and sugar. Then add egg, mashed bananas, and vanilla extract until well combined. Set aside.
2. Preheat the Air Fryer, adjust temperature to 300°F.
3. Sift together the flour, baking soda, and salt.
4. Fold the dry ingredients into the wet until combined. Mix in the chopped walnuts.
5. Grease the mini loaf pan with cooking spray, then fill with batter. Place into the preheated air fryer.
6. Select the Bake function, adjust time to 40 minutes.
7. Done and serve.

Puff Pastry Cinnamon Swirls

SERVINGS
9

TIME
25 min

DIFFICULTY
Medium

INGREDIENTS

- 1 egg for egg wash
- 1 sheet puff pastry thawed
- 1 cup brown sugar
- 1 teaspoon orange zest
- 1/2 cup salted butter softened
- 1 tablespoon cinnamon
- 1 teaspoon coarse sea salt
- 1 tablespoon coarse sugar to sprinkle on top

Orange Glaze
- 1/4 cup orange juice
- 2 cups powdered sugar
- 2 tablespoons cream
- 1 teaspoon orange zest

Puff Pastry Cinnamon Swirls
(CONTINUE)

DIRECTIONS

1. In a bowl, combine the butter, brown sugar, cinnamon, and orange zestand mix to combine. Spread the cinnamon sugar mixture on top of the puff pastry.
2. Gently roll up the edges and continue rolling, lightly moisten the edges with water or a but of egg wash to make them stick.
3. Using a sharp knife, cut puff pastry in 1 to 1.5" pieces. Then put the pieces on a parchment paper lined baking sheet.
4. Brush the tops of the pastry with the egg wash, then sprinkle with the coarse sugar and sea salt.
5. Bake the cinnamon swirls for 20-25 minutes in 350F degrees or until golden brown. The cinnamon sugar mixture will have leaked into the pan, but that it ok.
6. Remove and spoon the melted cinnamon sugar mixture from the pan over the top of the cinnamon swirls. Let cool for 5 minutes and the bottom will be perfectly caramelized with the cinnamon, sugar and butter mixture.
7. Drizzle with the orange glaze and serve. (Orange Glaze: Combine the orange juice, orange zest, cream and powdered sugar in a bowl and mix to combine)

Pineapple Squash Bread

SERVINGS
1 Medium Loaf

TIME
25 min

DIFFICULTY
Easy

INGREDIENTS

- 275 grams Strong bread flour.
- 1 1/2 tsp Instant dry yeast.
- 2 tbsp Warm water.
- 250 grams Squash puree.
- 1/4 tsp Chili powder.
- 1/2 tsp Salt.
- 1 tbsp Olive oil.
- 1/2 tbsp Curry powder.
- 1 tbsp Cumin.

DIRECTIONS

1. Whisk together warm water and yeast with a mixer. Let stand for 10 minutes to create foam.
2. Mix the squash puree into the flour until it resembles fine breadcrumbs. When yeast is ready, put flour into the bowl and add salt, spices, and oil.
3. Mix and knead until the dough is soft and elastic.
4. Transfer dough into an oiled bowl and let it stand to rise for 1 hour or until doubled in size.
5. Sprinkle flour into loaf tins. Knead the dough again briefly this time with the pineapple chunks and form into a loaf shape. Let stand for 1 hour.
6. Preheat Instant Air Fryer to 190oC.
7. Bake the loaf for 25 minutes.

Nutella Puff Pastry

SERVINGS
4

TIME
25 min

DIFFICULTY
Easy

INGREDIENTS

- 1/2 cup Nutella.
- 1 sheet puff pastry.
- 1 banana, sliced in 1.25" pieces

DIRECTIONS

1. Thaw the puff pastry according to the package instructions.
2. Preheat oven to 380 degrees F.
3. Cut the pastry into 9 squares using a sharp knife. On four squares, place a slice of banana and 2 teaspoons of Nutella on top of the banana.
4. Place the other 4 squares on top and seal the edges. Ensure that the edges are sealed well to avoid leaking while cooking.
5. Bake on a baking sheet for 10-15 minutes, or until light golden brown.
6. Let cool then serve.

Apple Bread

SERVINGS
6

TIME
50 min

DIFFICULTY
Medium

INGREDIENTS

- 2 eggs.
- 3 cups apples, cored and cubed.
- 1 tablespoon apple pie spice.
- 1 cup sugar.
- 2 cups white flour.
- 1 tablespoon vanilla.
- 1 stick butter.
- 1 tablespoon baking powder.
- 1 cup water.

DIRECTIONS

1. Mix egg with 1 butter stick, apple pie spice and sugar in a bowl and stir using mixer.
2. Add apples to the above mixture and stir again well.
3. In second bowl, mix baking powder with flour and stir.
4. Combine the 2 mixtures, stir and pour into a spring form pan.
5. Put spring form pan in your air fryer and cook at 320 degrees F for 40 minutes.
6. Slice and serve.

Garlic Bread

SERVINGS
12

TIME
25 min

DIFFICULTY
Medium

INGREDIENTS

- 10 tablespoons unsalted butter softened to room temperature.
- 8-10 garlic cloves minced (5-6 tablespoons).
- 1 baguette sliced into 1.25" slices.
- 1/2 teaspoon black pepper.
- 1 teaspoon salt.
- 1 teaspoon Italian seasoning.
- Shredded mozzarella option for cheesy bread.

DIRECTIONS

1. In a bowl, mix the butter, garlic, pepper, salt and Italian seasoning to combine, then spread mixture on the slices of bread.
2. Place in the air fryer in a single layer (you'll need to do several batches).
3. Cook at 350 degrees F for 5-7 minutes. Start checking at 4 minutes for doneness.
4. To make cheesy bread, once the garlic bread has cooked for 4-5 minutes, remove and top with meltable cheese. Bake for another 1-2 minutes, until the cheese is lightly browned and melted.

Orange Blossoms Bread

SERVINGS	TIME	DIFFICULTY
24 rolls	50 min	Medium

INGREDIENTS

- Rolls
- 1 large egg
- 1/2 cup (113g) water, lukewarm
- 1/2 cup (113g) orange juice, lukewarm
- 1/2 cup (113g) sour cream, at room temperature
- 1.25 teaspoons (8g) salt
- 1/3 cup (74g) granulated sugar
- 1 tablespoon orange zest (grated rind) or 1/2 teaspoon orange oil
- 4.25 cups (510g) All-Purpose Flour
- 2 teaspoons instant yeast.

Glaze
- 1 cup (113g) confectioners' sugar.
- 1.5 to 2 tablespoons orange juice.

Orange Blossoms Bread
(CONTINUE)

DIRECTIONS

1. Make the dough: measure it by gently spooning it into a cup, then sweeping off any excess.combine the ingredients in the order listed and mix until soft, smooth dough forms. Turn the dough out on a lightly floured surface ad knead it for 7 minutes, or knead in a stand mixer at medium for 5 minutes. The dough should be soft but not sticky.
2. Place the dough in a greased bowl, cover, and let rise for 1 to 1 1/2 hours; it'll be puffy.
3. Deflate the dough and turn it out onto a greased work surface. Divide it into 24 golf ball-sized pieces, about 1 3/8 ounces (39g) each. Roll the dough into balls, and place into two greased 9" round cake pans.
4. Cover the pans with lightly greased plastic wrap and allow let rise at room temperature for 1 1/2 hours, until puffy. (If desired, snip a cross in the top of each roll in a star pattern, cutting 1/2" deep, to make "petals.")
5. Toward the end of the rise, preheat the Air Fryer to 350°F. Bake the rolls for 20 to 23 minutes, or until they're a light, golden brown.
6. Remove from the oven, and Let cool in the pan for 10 minutes before transferring the rolls to a rack to finish cooling completely.
7. To make the glaze: Combine the sugar and orange juice until smooth; drizzle the glaze over the lukewarm rolls.

Strawberry Pie

SERVINGS
12

TIME
30 min

DIFFICULTY
Medium

INGREDIENTS

For the crust:
- 1 cup coconut, shredded.
- 1 cup sunflower seeds.
- 1/4 cup butter.

For the filling:
- 1/2 cup heavy cream.
- 1 teaspoon gelatin.
- 1/2 tablespoon lemon juice.
- 4 ounces strawberries.
- 8 ounces cream cheese.
- 2 tablespoons water.
- 1/4 teaspoon stevia.
- 8 ounces strawberries, chopped for serving.

DIRECTIONS

1. Mix sunflower seeds with coconut, a pinch of salt and butter in your food processor, pulse and press this on the bottom of a cake pan that fits your air fryer.
2. Heat up a pan with the water over medium heat, add gelatin, stir until it dissolves, leave aside to cool down, add this to your food processor, mix with 4 ounces strawberries, cream cheese, lemon juice and stevia and blend well.
3. Add heavy cream, stir well and spread this over crust.
4. Top with 8 ounces strawberries, introduce in your air fryer and cook at 330 degrees F for 15-18 minutes.
5. Keep in the fridge until serve

Pumpkin Pie

SERVINGS
6

TIME
25 min

DIFFICULTY
Medium

INGREDIENTS

- 1 tablespoon sugar.
- 2 tablespoons water.
- 1 tablespoon butter.
- 2 tablespoons flour.

For the pumpkin pie filling:
- 3.5 ounces pumpkin flesh, chopped.
- 1 egg, whisked.
- 1 teaspoon mixed spice.
- 1 tablespoon sugar.
- 1 teaspoon nutmeg.
- 3 ounces water.

DIRECTIONS

1. Put 3 ounces water in a pot, bring to a boil over medium heat, add pumpkin, egg, 1 tablespoon sugar, spice and nutmeg, stir, boil for 20 minutes, take off heat.
2. Blend the above mixture in a blender.
3. Mix flour with butter, 1 tablespoon sugar and 2 tablespoons water in a bowl and knead your dough well.
4. Grease a pie pan that fits your air fryer with butter, Put dough into the pan, fill with pumpkin pie filling, place in your air fryer's basket and bake at 360 degrees F for 15-18 minutes.
5. Slice and serve warm.

Peach Pie

SERVINGS	TIME	DIFFICULTY
4	40 min	Medium

INGREDIENTS

- 1 pie dough.
- 2 tablespoons butter, melted.
- 2.25 pounds peaches, pitted and chopped.
- 1/2 cup sugar.
- 2 tablespoons cornstarch.
- A pinch of nutmeg, ground.
- 2 tablespoons flour.
- 1 tablespoon dark rum.
- 1 tablespoon lemon juice.

DIRECTIONS

1. Mix peaches with cornstarch, sugar, flour, nutmeg, rum, lemon juice and butter in a bowl and stir well.
2. Roll pie dough into a pie pan that fits your air fryer and press well.
3. Pour and spread mixture in step 1 into pie pan, introduce in your air fryer and bake at 350 degrees F for 35 minutes.
4. Serve warm or cold.

Lentils and Dates Brownies

SERVINGS
2

TIME
15 min

DIFFICULTY
Easy

INGREDIENTS

- 4 tablespoons almond butter.
- 1 banana, peeled and chopped.
- 28 ounces canned lentils, rinsed and drained.
- 12 dates.
- 1 tablespoon honey.
- 1/2 teaspoon baking soda.
- 2 tablespoons cocoa powder.

DIRECTIONS

1. Mix lentils with butter, banana, cocoa, baking soda, honey in your food processor and blend really well.
2. Add dates, pulse a few more times, pour this into a greased pan that fits your air fryer, spread evenly.
3. Introduce in the fryer at 360 degrees F and bake for 17 minutes.
4. Take brownies mix out of the oven, cut, arrange on a platter and serve.

Vanilla Brownies

SERVINGS
8

TIME
20 min

DIFFICULTY
Easy

INGREDIENTS

- 1/2 cup condensed milk.
- 1 tbsp unsalted butter (softened or melted).
- 3 tbsp vanilla essence.
- 2 tbsp water.
- 1/2 cup chopped nuts (use mixed nuts if you prefer)
- 2 cups all-purpose flour (split it up as half a cup, 2 tbsp and 1 tsp)

DIRECTIONS

1. Mix the ingredients together and beat until you get a smooth mixture.
2. Grease tin with butter, Preheat fryer to 300 degrees F for five minutes.
3. Pour batter into tin and place in preheated air fryer, bake at 300 degrees F for 5 minutes. Check that the brownies are done with a knife or toothpick and remove the tray.
4. When the macaroons have cooled, cut them and serve with a scoop of ice cream.

Printed in Great Britain
by Amazon